A Director's
Guide to
Stanislavsky's
Active Analysis

A Director's Guide to Stanislavsky's Active Analysis

Including the Formative Essay on Active Analysis by Maria Knebel

JAMES THOMAS

Bloomsbury Methuen Drama
An imprint of Bloomsbury Publishing Plc

BLOOMSBURY
LONDON · OXFORD · NEW YORK · NEW DELHI · SYDNEY

Bloomsbury Methuen Drama

An imprint of Bloomsbury Publishing Plc

50 Bedford Square	1385 Broadway
London	New York
WC1B 3DP	NY 10018
UK	USA

www.bloomsbury.com

Bloomsbury is a registered trade mark of Bloomsbury Publishing Plc

First published 2016
Reprinted 2017

Copyright © James Thomas 2016

Excerpt from *Shkola Borisa Zona* (*The School of Boris Zon*), courtesy of Séance Publishers,
St Petersburg © 2011

British Library Cataloguing-in-Publication Data

A catalogue record for this book is available from the British Library.

ISBN:	HB:	978-1-4742-5658-2
	PB:	978-1-4742-5659-9
	ePDF:	978-1-4742-5660-5
	ePub:	978-1-4742-5662-9

Library of Congress Cataloging-in-Publication Data

Names: Thomas, James, 1943- author. | Knebel§, M. (Mariëiìa). O dejstvennom analize p'esy
i roli. English.
Title: A director's guide to Stanislavsky's active analysis : including the formative essay on
active analysis by Maria Knebel / by James Thomas.
Description: London : New York : Bloomsbury Methuen Drama, 2016. | Includes the first
English translation of Maria Knebel's foundational article about active analysis, originally
published: Moscow: Iskusstvo, 1959, under the title: O dejstvennom analize p'esy i roli. |
Includes bibliographical references.
Identifiers: LCCN 2015047539| ISBN 9781474256599 (pbk.) | ISBN 9781474256582
(hardback)
Subjects: LCSH: Theater rehearsals. | Theater–Production and direction. | Method acting. |
Stanislavsky, Konstantin, 1863-1938–Criticism and interpretation.
Classification: LCC PN2071.R45.T57 2016 | DDC 792.02/8–dc23 LC record available at
http://lccn.loc.gov/2015047539

Cover design: Eleanor Rose

Typeset by RefineCatch Limited, Bungay, Suffolk
Printed and bound in Great Britain

The Method of Active Analysis is in my opinion the most perfect method of work with the actor, the crowning achievement of Stanislavsky's lifelong search in the sphere of methodology.

– GEORGII TOVSTONOGOV, *THE PROFESSION OF STAGE DIRECTOR*

Contents

Acknowledgements

I am grateful to Wayne State University for the Murray Jackson Creative Scholar in the Arts Award, which provided the time and financial support necessary for this book.

Thanks also go to my students – Carl Ghigliazza, Michael Gingerella, Shannon Hurst, Danté Jones, Taylor Morrow, Anna Seibert, Maria Simpkins and Graham Todd – for their involvement in the Active Analysis workshops for *A Midsummer Night's Dream*. I owe special thanks to Matt Foss and Jennifer Goff for their helpful comments on the early drafts.

Here as well I would like to thank Seance Publishers of St Petersburg, Russia, for permission to translate passages from *Shkola Boris Zona* by Boris Zon, St Petersburg, RU: St Petersburg Theatre Institute, 2011.

Finally yet importantly, I am indebted to Dmitry Krymov for permission to draw from the writings of his father, the legendary Russian director Anatoly Efros.

Preface

Konstantin Stanislavsky (1863–1938) is the most influential and least understood, the most cited and, probably for that reason, one of the least read figures in the panoply of great theatre artists. His ideas have transformed acting and directing throughout much of the world and have contributed to the psychological depth and continuing vitality of the modern theatre as a whole. His ideas are also blamed for scores of the modern theatre's excesses and eccentricities that have arisen since his time. Moreover, since there has been a wide range of writings about Stanislavsky from many different perspectives, he has consequently been appropriated by many people, including entire academic and performance disciplines, schools of theatre, and aesthetic agendas – all to serve their own purposes. Nevertheless, Stanislavsky remains for the most part a respectable ancestor, but one whom too few actors, directors, or designers still read.

With such a fragmented and sometimes self-contradictory heritage, where can we find an account of Stanislavsky that we can trust, that sketches his ideas and traces their development, with proper reckoning of his time, place, and professional associations? A worthwhile place to start would be the writings by and about his work that have emerged since 1991, following the collapse of the Soviet Union and the subsequent opening of the Moscow Art Theatre archives to researchers from the West. These post-Soviet writings in their totality represent the most creditable English-language discussions of the full range of Stanislavsky's ideas, balancing the demands of scholars for precision and all the scholarly apparatus with the demands for an account that serves the practical needs of the stage. Chief among these are the new translations of Stanislavsky's major works by Jean Benedetti, in addition to the writings of Sharon Carnicke, Sergei Tcherkasski, Robert Leach, David Chambers, Bella Merlin and Jonathan Pitches. Important as well are the books of the legendary Russian director Anatoly Efros (1925–1987), whose productions and writings form a crucial link between Stanislavsky's ideas and contemporary practice.[1]

Some of the most important information that has emerged since 1991 concerns Stanislavsky's final work, the Method of Active Analysis, or as it was misnamed at first, the Method of Physical Actions.[2] He devoted his last years to its development, and it comprises the summary of his life's work. The translations and writings noted above provide excellent explanations of this innovative practice. With the exception of Efros's books, however, the target readers tend to be actors and theatre scholars, not necessarily directors or directing teachers as such. Yet, in my view, it is of the greatest importance that directors should understand the value of this late movement in Stanislavsky's thinking – a movement beyond the actor's work on him/herself and towards a new type of rehearsal process, with associated changes in the role of the director. The more a director knows about these questions, the more he/she will be ready to offer the deepest and most sensitive support to actors and designers. This book is intended to fill that gap through a sustained treatment of Active Analysis *from a director's point of view.*

Much of the systematic writing about directing has tended to deal with the 'objective' tradition (the text of the play dominates the style and practice) developed by the Moscow Art Theatre and probably the most widely in practice today. Additionally, directors in the 'virtuoso' tradition (the distinctive style and practice dominates the text) of Vsevolod Meyerhold, Jerzy Grotowski and Peter Brook have made substantial contributions of their own.[3] Much has also been written by them and about their work, and as a result, their characteristic approaches have become available to the wider theatre community as well. Active Analysis accommodates itself to all sorts of directorial viewpoints. Nevertheless, it is important to emphasize that the attention given to this method does not imply that other approaches are less creative, less effective, or less valid. I have simply agreed to set them aside for the time being in favour of explaining Active Analysis. No single approach to play directing and rehearsal can ever be considered the best, of course, but I hope to convince readers that a large number of playable dramatic values can be discovered using this approach.

Regarding the arrangement rather than the subject, this book is intended to accommodate different reading, learning and teaching strategies. It is purposely organized deductively, that is, from the application of Active Analysis in the first part to its theoretical basis in the second part. First, by the *how* of Active Analysis and *how* its application can lead to fresh contemporary outcomes for a well-known play, and only after that, by explaining the *what,* the theoretical principles upon which Active Analysis is based. The objective is to avoid taxing the patience of readers with too much abstract thinking at the outset. On the other hand, there is no compelling reason to follow this arrangement. Some readers may choose to read the theory before the practice; others may reference the headings to mix and interweave content from both parts; and still others may decide to use the book as a supplement for other approaches to directing. Nevertheless, a great deal can be gained, I think, by dealing with the book in its present configuration.

Introduction

The first part of this book is based on my experience with Active Analysis on stage and in the studio for more than twenty years, on ideas drawn from nearly two decades of classes and discussions with master teachers at the Moscow Art Theatre School, and from Russian stage performances too numerous to mention. Most of all, the first part has been influenced by the work of the Russian director Anatoly Efros (1925–1987). Although I never had the good fortune to meet Efros, I mainly acquired my knowledge and understanding of Active Analysis through translating his books, talking with his students and followers, and from my own practical work based on these encounters.[1] This is not to say the new translations of Stanislavsky and appraisals of his final work have been any less valuable for me. In important ways, they clarified and enhanced my understanding of ideas I acquired initially from Efros. That being said, none of the errors in Part 1 should be attributed to Efros, although much of what is sound and helpful can be traced to his influence.

My first effort at explaining Active Analysis focused on its intellectual features. I collected them under the label of Action Analysis and included them in my book on play analysis.[2] Although I also included a few general remarks in there about the practice of Active Analysis, I avoided talking about its applied features because the scope of that book was intended to be exclusively analytical. A few features of Action Analysis are included in Part 1 here, but in this book I attempt to organize ideas and practices that have been saved up for years in my directing and teaching. Therefore, Part 1 is more like a directorial case study in the form of a textbook, but also containing notes and a bibliography for scholarly requirements. The interpretation of *A Midsummer Night's Dream* put forward in Part 1 was developed in my Active Analysis workshops, and how those experiences worked themselves out is considered here. The first part of the book is intended mainly to serve as an illustration, however, rather than a proof. In other words, Active Analysis as an approach to directing should not necessarily be faulted if there are flaws in the interpretation of the play derived from it here. Since Active Analysis is essentially a rehearsal method, a systematic first-hand account of this type, I think, can be especially useful for directors. After all, they are the ones who most need to understand the distinctive mode of thinking that accompanies Active Analysis in the sphere of play production.

The second part of this book addresses Active Analysis in and of itself. What are the precise circumstances, ideas and methods associated with Stanislavsky's ultimate work? Fortunately, besides the important writings of the authors named above, we also have the first-hand account of Maria Knebel (1898–1985), who was one of Stanislavsky's personal students in the final years of his life. Not only that, Knebel had considerable standing of her own in the profession. First, as an actor and director at the Moscow Art Theatre, then as Chief Director of the Central Children's Theatre, where the rebirth of the Russian theatre began after the death of Joseph Stalin. Perhaps most important, Knebel was also Master Teacher of Directing at the State Institute for Theatre Training in Moscow (GITIS, now RATI), during which time she authored influential books on the pedagogy of directing. Anatoly Efros was one her students, and for many Russians then and now his productions epitomized Active Analysis in post-Stanislavsky theatre practice.

In a 1952 article titled 'Vysokaya Prostota' [Superior Simplicity] published in Russia's leading theatre periodical, *Teatr,* Knebel wrote about an important conference that took place earlier that year in Moscow.[3] She reported that a group of prominent Russian actors and directors had met formally to talk about the experimental rehearsal method Stanislavsky developed during the last years of his life. Rumors about a puzzling change in Stanislavsky's thinking during his final years had passed around in Russian theatre circles ever since his death in 1938. However, the new method of work remained largely undefined until this historic meeting.

This lack of definition was for reasons both in and outside of Stanislavsky. Ultimately, everything known about Stanislavsky's final work at that time came from his incomplete works, a few paragraphs published here and there by his personal students, isolated oral accounts, and the practical training done at his Opera and Drama Studio.[4] Furthermore, in the years following Stanislavsky's death, his students went their separate ways, making use of their teacher's principles in keeping with their own requirements.[5] Knebel felt this situation had unintentionally contributed to an alteration of Stanislavsky's original ideas, some of which, she said, had become seriously distorted in the process of adoption. Another source of confusion was Stanislavsky's way of constantly testing and revising his initial assumptions, a practice that resulted in long intervals between publications of his books.

According to Knebel, within a short time after Stanislavsky's death his followers found themselves divided into three distinct if informal factions. One faction believed that all of Stanislavsky's teachings were summed up in the so-called Method of Physical Actions and its associated ideas and practices. Another favoured the term Method of Active Analysis and a different set of ideas and practices. A third believed that Stanislavsky's importance resulted primarily from his earliest work, notably the well-known emotion memory, through-action, communion (communication), units (pieces) and objectives (tasks). Knebel belonged to the group that favoured Active Analysis. The participants of the conference identified and clarified these differences, but, as Knebel implied, they apparently fell short of harmonizing them. Thus, Stanislavsky's final teachings, the culmination of his life's work, continued to remain in question outside a small group of his personal students.

Knebel set out to change this situation through her writing and teaching. In the *Teatr* article, she briefly introduced Stanislavsky's breakthrough, explaining it as an approach to play analysis and rehearsal based on the natural processes and distinct individualities of the actor's own imagination. Drawing from discussions at the conference, Knebel acknowledged that at first it seemed to her and others that Stanislavsky had completely rejected his former principles. He seemed to be abandoning, for instance, the practice of lengthy concentrated study of the play text during the first period of rehearsal, a practice that became the intellectual foundation of his work and that of Nemirovich-Danchenko at the Moscow Art Theatre. However, succeeding practice convinced Knebel that the new technique was solidly built on everything Stanislavsky had discovered earlier. Today, though, many directors and actors in the English-speaking theatre are still unclear about Stanislavsky's final work. After all, the Moscow Art Theatre had instilled in its followers an absolute reverence for its own special manner of analysis and rehearsal – extensive text analysis 'at the table', followed by a period of physical embodiment. Experience had proven this approach capable of producing consistently good, at times even brilliant results. In contrast, Stanislavsky himself came to believe the rehearsal process that he and Nemirovich-Danchenko developed had become outdated, even creatively harmful. Regrettably, Stanislavsky was unable to muster the strength necessary to record his late discoveries in writing or attempt to reorient the veteran actors of his own theatre. Thus, he decided to bestow the legacy of his new findings on a carefully selected group of apprentice directors. Maria Knebel was chief among those he personally chose for this purpose.

Stanislavsky's goal, Knebel reminded her readers, had always been to find a way to release the creative individuality of actors, to encourage them to take personal responsibility for their creative work, and to arouse their own psychological and physical resources. She explained that in his new work he was determined to avoid the pitfalls of memorizing a dramatic text by rote and to escape the artificial division between internal and external work. In her article, she only hinted at what Stanislavsky's new method might have involved. She was concerned that a condensed account might be misemployed as a solution to all the actor's creative problems. After all, she said, for those who are only concerned with results, it might seem that this new technique could be mastered with tempting ease. Taken all together, Stanislavsky's system could be considered as something bulky and immense, whereas at first glance Active Analysis appears to be tidy and manageable. It is only necessary to master its comparatively small number of principles and everything else becomes simple and clear. Knebel insisted that such thinking was deeply mistaken. Active Analysis does not remove or abridge anything from Stanislavsky's earlier work, but on the contrary, collects it all together and summarizes it. Not only does Active Analysis incorporate all of Stanislavsky's previous work but also it provides a methodology for making the most of that work in real-world rehearsal and performance. Without understanding this key fact, it is hard to appreciate the long-term significance of his breakthrough.

In 1959, Knebel set down in writing all she had learned about Stanislavsky's final work in a monograph titled *O dejstvennom analize p'esy i roli* [Active Analysis of the Play and the Role].[6] Not surprisingly, her article is enormously instructive; it is also rather verbose, containing numerous digressions about Russian drama and Soviet-Russian theatre with which Western readers may not have had much experience. In 1971, she prepared a revised version and included it with some of her other writings in *O tom, chto mne kazhetsâ osobenno vazhnym* [What is Especially Important to Me].[7] This version is more concise and less specifically 'Soviet-Russian.' My translation of this version comprises Part 2 of this book.

PART ONE

A Director's Work with Active Analysis

1

Choosing the Play

We are about to study the work of a stage director using Stanislavsky's Method of Active Analysis. Since it is usually better to carry out this kind of study in practical terms, we will select a single play and set down the process of work on it from the beginning up to technical rehearsals. First, we will look at the intellectual components of Active Analysis by undertaking a systematic study of the play itself. Next, we will look at the practice of Active Analysis in rehearsal. In this way, a specific and concrete discussion of the entire process is possible.

We will start by choosing a play. What kind of play? Historical, modern, avant-garde, new work? Some directors prefer historical; others, early modern plays; others, contemporary plays or new plays; and still others make their choices from a wide range of periods and styles. As important as play selection is, however, directors also tend to be drawn to works in which life is reflected with both psychological depth and immediate relevance. Many directors think that Shakespeare's plays make these goals possible – to be faithful to the author's text, to understand it accurately, and furthermore to express one's own ideas about our time, our society, and our audiences.

It is always interesting when a director re-envisions one of the works of the past or when a director formulates an innovative approach to a classic play, such as those of Sophocles, Moliere, or Shakespeare.[1] Yet, the decision to do a classic play also ought to have a fresh, up-to-date, imaginative point of view about it, something beyond traditional formulas. For a director, this undertaking requires working truly and deeply, first to detect and then to express a pulse of modernity in the play. Not merely external relevance, so-called updating, but something deeply and fittingly important for today, here, and now. If this does not take place, then a classic production, especially under less-than-ideal conditions, can often seem like a museum piece or a costume party.

Even under ideal conditions, the production of a classic play is not easy. In a modern play, life as written is closer to us and consequently easier to understand. In addition, of course, it is far easier to direct and act a play from one's own time than one from Shakespeare's time. Equally important, today's audiences already see many excellent contemporary plays, films and (recently) television programmes about our times and our society. Nonetheless, audiences generally look forward to a play that thoughtfully addresses the questions of the here and now, a truthful expression of life today, no matter what the period was in which it was written.

One of these classics, and one that always seems to touch a chord with contemporary audiences, is Shakespeare's play, *A Midsummer Night's Dream* (henceforth *Midsummer*). It is not chosen here because it is ideal in terms of its structure or meaning or because the interpretation put forward is startlingly original. But mainly because it contains a life-affirming heart with the potential to provide an interesting performance and – this is the key – one that is relevant to the present day. *Midsummer* has a direct relationship to contemporary life, I think, because it involves a number of present-day concerns: imagination, ego representations and power, gender role strain, sexual repression and personal transformation, patriarchy, class structures, the constraints of language, and even environmentalism. These concerns combine to produce an incredible confusion of relationships in this play. The characters make a mass of mistakes by unthinkingly imposing their ideas on others, especially their ideas about women and love. For our practical purposes here, a final point of importance is the fact that *Midsummer* also contains a wide range of scenes and roles useful for study and practice.

One director's interpretation of a masterpiece by Shakespeare may differ greatly from another's, may even be diametrically opposed, and at the same time be valid, if only for demonstration purposes. Thus, the ideas about *Midsummer* that follow should not be understood simply as an aid for those wishing to direct it. In any case, the ideas are not startlingly original, nor are they intended to be authoritative in any way. The discussion of *Midsummer* that follows is concerned primarily about the director's work with Active Analysis.

Plot summary of *A Midsummer Night's Dream*

This book uses a single study play, though its text is not reproduced here; it is meant to accompany a copy of the play. The following summary is provided as an aid to the reader's memory.

There are four plots. The first, which 'frames' the play, concerns the marriage of Theseus, Duke of Athens, and Hippolyta, Queen of the Amazons and his bride-to-be. The play begins in Theseus's palace, and during the first scene, we learn about his plans for their forthcoming wedding. Theseus is a wise Duke. Although formerly a womanizer, nevertheless he seems quite inexperienced about the nature of true love. Hippolyta is an affectionate if understandably reticent bride, whom he honestly, if naively, loves and therefore wishes to impress.

The second and main plot is the story of four young Athenian lovers, Lysander and Hermia along with Demetrius and Helena. All four are described as Athenian youths. Hermia's father, Egeus, comes before Theseus with a complaint about his daughter. He has chosen Demetrius to be her husband, but she prefers Lysander. Being the ruler, Theseus must observe a father's legal rights, and so he orders Hermia to obey her father's wishes, otherwise she will face death or enforced virginal life as a priestess. All the same, Hermia does not wish to surrender to threats where her feelings are concerned.

In a short scene where Hermia and Lysander are alone, they decide to run away together. They will get married at the home of his rich widow aunt, who lives on the other side of the woods, safely out of the reach of Athenian law. Before preparing to depart, they disclose their plan to Helena, Hermia's closest friend and recently the jilted lover of Demetrius. Inspired by her friend's bravery, Helena comes up with a brave plan of her own. She will inform Demetrius what Hermia and Lysander are up to, and when he follows them into the woods to stop them, she will follow him there, where she will attempt to win him back.

Next, another group of characters appear, the third plot. A group of Athenian artisans has gathered at the home of their organizer to cast a play they hope to perform for the Duke's wedding celebrations. Simple, unaffected characters, they treat the business of casting and rehearsal with great seriousness. After a certain amount of bickering over the distribution of roles, they make plans to meet in the woods next day to rehearse.

A fourth plot emerges when we learn that these woods have a ruler of their own, Oberon, King of the Fairies and someone to whom all the spirits of the woods are subject. In addition, just as Duke Theseus demands obedience to the customs and laws of Athens, so also King Oberon employs magic and spells to subordinate others to the customs and laws of the fairy world. This is how he punishes his wife Titania, Queen of the Fairies, who has disagreed with him about the upbringing of their adoptive son. She wishes to keep him beside her to preserve the memory of the boy's mother, who was her closest friend, while Theseus thinks it is time for the boy to be with his father and start growing up. Accordingly, Oberon instructs his sprite-servant, Puck, to fetch some flowers, whose nectar, when rubbed in a sleeper's eyes, will arouse love-at-first-sight when the sleeper awakes. Oberon will use this nectar on Titania, and when she falls in love with some ridiculous forest creature, he will refuse to remove the spell until she agrees to hand the boy over to him.

With the introduction of the magic nectar into the story, the second, third and fourth plot lines begin to overlap, leading to a series of complex events caused by the use and misuse of the nectar on various characters. In a sequence of brilliantly orchestrated episodes, the lovers switch their affections so that Lysander and Demetrius fall in love with Helena, while Hermia is left out of the picture – the exact reverse of their relations at the beginning of the play. Additionally, Titania falls in love with Bottom, whose head Puck has mischievously transformed into that of an ass. Of course, the nectar's victims are not aware that the cause of their new affections is not in themselves but in Oberon's magic. These episodes form the dramatic and thematic heart of the play.

Shakespeare unravels all this confusion and returns to the first plot rapidly and matter-of-factly, as is his habit. While Titania is under the spell of the nectar, Oberon recovers their son (offstage), and Titania is left with only a shadowy recollection of her enchantment with Bottom. Oberon reverses the effects of the nectar on the lovers, and, when they awake, Lysander is reconciled with Hermia and Demetrius with Helena. Bottom is also returned to his normal state. At this point, Theseus, Hippolyta and Egeus enter on a morning excursion prior to the wedding celebrations later that day. They happen upon the lovers just at the moment when they awaken from their spell. After hearing about the extraordinary events of the previous night, Theseus overrules Egeus's original demand and invites the lovers to the royal wedding, where the two young couples will be married along with Theseus and Hippolyta. Like Titania, the young lovers and Bottom are left with only a vague recollection of their drug-induced adventures in the woods.

In the final scene of the play, the Mechanicals entertain the three pairs of newly married lovers with an earnest if amateurish performance of the classic love story, *Pyramus and Thisbe*, while their audience responds with sympathetic if ironic amusement. When the lovers retire, Oberon and Titania arrive to bless the nuptials, and Puck adds a clever note of farewell directly to the audience.

2

Director's Plan: General Challenges

As with any other approach to directing, the first phase of work with Active Analysis intellectual homework involves the so-called director's plan. This plan will inevitably change and improve while at the same time growing more complete and specific as the director begins rehearsing with the actors. Also identical to similar endeavours, the director's plan for Active Analysis begins by addressing a few general questions about the play, and is then followed by study that is more specific. There is a difference, however: Active Analysis employs a point of view that corresponds with Stanislavsky's psychophysical approach to acting. Consequently, since awareness of Stanislavsky's system needs to be present in every paragraph, the questions to ask and how to answer them become quite important.

Director's impression[1]

As the term is used here, 'director's impression' refers to an idea, feeling, or opinion arising from the director's initial readings of a play. The director's impression should not be confused with an undeveloped 'vision' of the future production. Vision is the faculty or state of being able to *see*. And a vision is undeveloped when it is based on impulse rather than sustained thought. Nor should the director's impression be confused with the 'production concept', which is an original idea or plan for expressing a play and governing its entire production. Of course, it is completely natural to allow the director's visual imagination free play in the process of reading a play; many directors consider this one of the main features of their work. Some directors may go so far as to adopt their visual impression as the basis for a production concept, but that is not how the terms are meant to be understood here. A director's *vision* is a quick visual image of the play, or scenes from the play, that happens to come to mind. Typically, it is pedestrian and filled with clichés precisely because it is impulsive and superficial. It may even be introduced into the mise-en-scène and thereby become visually expressive, but this makes little difference. The director in this instance has not gone much further than the ordinary visions expected of any layperson who reads a play.

In contrast, the director's *impression* is unique and critically important for a director specifically. One director may obtain an impression that is largely rhythmic; another, an impression in which sounds or colours or shapes dominate; still another, an impression of a sharp social idea or a cluster of emotional feelings; sometimes the impression is even a simple piece of furniture, a flower, a scent, a painting, etc. When one well-known director began to read Ibsen's *Hedda Gabler* in preparation for a production, he received the impression of a comfortable, well-worn Victorian easy chair from his own home, and this impression eventually led to a genuinely innovative interpretation. Moreover, that very chair was used in the production. Stanislavsky and Michael Chekhov considered the director's impression to be an essential part of the creative process and they recommended writing it down to retain its undiluted freshness. There is no need to try to give such impressions an exact verbal formulation, however. Initially, it is enough for the director to write down the first internal impression, even though it may initially be expressed in fairly vague terms.

Why write it down? Mainly because a director's impression can gradually fade from memory during the chaos of rehearsals. If the impression is written down, the director can always check to see if what is happening in rehearsals matches up with what was initially intuited about the play or if rehearsals have wandered in some other direction. The impression could be one of an atmosphere, for example, 'expectation', 'disappointment', or 'sunshine on a cloudy day'. This director's impression for *Midsummer* was the mood created by Hippolyta's line: '... something of great constancy; / But, howsoever, *strange and admirable.*' (5.1.27–28, italics added). If rehearsals or near-final results fail to produce the atmosphere of 'expectation', 'disappointment', or 'sunshine on a cloudy day', or in the case of our *Midsummer*, fail to express the spirit of Hippolyta's line, then it is likely that the director's creative path is off course. Conversely, if the director's initial and later impressions are in harmony, then the director is probably proceeding on a path that is in harmony with his/her creative imagination and therefore in harmony with the goals of Active Analysis.

Directorial impressions are not always correct either, of course. A director may assume one thing at the beginning and something completely different, although perhaps more acceptable, turns out at the end. Sometimes, in the intellectual homework phase, the director does not succeed in accurately grasping the full meaning of a play. This is particularly true with Shakespeare, whose plays carry an enormous weight of historical and theatrical baggage with which a director has to contend. Sometimes as well, a play's unusual setting or subject matter can be so striking as to conceal the meaning or hide the absence of coherent meaning. When a director reads a play and already 'sees' it on stage, however, this is not the type of impression to which Stanislavsky and Michael Chekhov referred. In their view and that of this book, the director who tries to grasp an emotional impression of the whole play ought to trust it as an impression in the strictest sense of the word, and then question it *with the actors* by way of Active Analysis at applicable points in rehearsal.

FURTHER THOUGHTS

Directors have their clichés just as actors do, only more so. They appear at the very beginning of work on a production, when the director puts his/her intellect and creative imagination to work analyzing the play. Many directors undervalue the importance of this period for the entire process of play production and rarely do directors make a serious effort to understand the workings of their own creative imaginations.

Try the following exercise. What visions appear with the following words: Shakespeare, forest, palace, fairies, love, Amazons, Athens and Mechanicals? If much the same visions appear to virtually everyone, what possible value could they have for a director? Audiences could obtain the same visions for themselves simply by reading the play. In some productions, the audiences may even be ahead of the director in this respect. The director's impression ought to go beyond that of the layperson. Otherwise, the theatre cannot claim to be the enriching experience on which its very identity as an independent art form depends.

Select one the secondary plots of *Midsummer* (Theseus and Hippolyta, the Mechanicals, Oberon and Titania). Read over the episodes of that plot more than a few times and each time at one sitting, nonstop and end-to-end. Make a note of any feelings, thoughts, impressions, and technical problems that come to mind, regardless of their apparent vagueness, illogic, or meaning. Then, for the time being, set aside any conclusive thinking about external forms, production concepts, and visions of the play and its future manifestation on stage. In particular, avoid hindering one's imagination at this point with material questions, such as 'Is it technically achievable?' Do write down impressions that are deeply rooted in one's creative imagination – free-floating sights, sounds, words and tactile sensations. These impressions may not always be found in the selected plot itself, nor need they be entirely coherent at this early stage of work. Nevertheless, they are the nourishment that feeds one's imagination and therefore the decisive source of the director's creative contribution to a production.

Internal plausibility

The director of *Midsummer* immediately faces a challenge that would be a cause for concern for any play containing such an exceedingly wide range of given circumstances. Namely, the challenge of *internal plausibility*.

The world of Theseus and Hippolyta, even though they are figures from classical mythology, is all the same presented as a world of recognizable human figures. For them, the question of internal plausibility would not be a cause for excessive concern. However, the world of Oberon and Titania – with its elves and fairies, magic spells and extreme transformations – this fantastical world definitely raises the question of internal plausibility.

Another challenge of internal plausibility is the play's well-known final scene, where, from a psychological perspective at least, Shakespeare does not seem to get means together with ends. The wedding celebration, the Mechanicals' performance, and the stage spectators' comments are all plausible enough on the surface. Yet to avoid lapsing into stereotypes and over-acting, these external matters ought to possess internal plausibility as well. In other words, the final scene needs to do more than conform to the expectations of a predictable Shakespearean comic ending. Somehow, it ought to be genuinely Shakespearean inside as well as outside. It needs to express a meaning as well as a story.

Theseus, Hippolyta, and Egeus are essential to the play's action, but they can become uninteresting and therefore problematic without internal plausibility beyond that of 'framing the action', as literary analysts might say. A similar challenge arises with the young lovers. Analysts often point out their apparent lack of individuality, given that they appear to be largely indistinguishable from one another apart from their names and genders. They fall in and out of love with each other in similar ways and under similar circumstances. Can this really be Shakespeare, or is something going on inside of them and inside the structure of the play that allows them to be more than the silly creatures they appear to be?

A further challenge of internal plausibility arises in performances of the non-realistic characters: Oberon, Titania and Puck. A typically challenging episode is that of Titania falling in love with Bottom bestowed with an ass's head. On the one hand, this is obviously a situation involving non-realistic characters in a non-realistic situation. Some directors have come to accept the inner life of these characters as similarly non-realistic, that is, psychologically implausible but nonetheless primitively entertaining. On the other hand, Stanislavsky, Meyerhold, Vakhtangov and Grotowski, among other well-known directors, have shown that such departures from realistic expectations require internal plausibility even so. Indeed, larger-than-life behaviour requires even more rigorous attention to internal plausibility than realism does. For in realism, internal plausibility is more recognizable because it is closer to that of everyday life.

Another general challenge comes from the language. In Shakespeare's time language had a greater importance than it has today. Language was a powerful way to express the emerging awareness of individualism that characterized Renaissance England. And in Shakespeare's plays, this individualism is essentially an experience of language. Nevertheless, the language of the young lovers, for example, puts one on guard. It seems overly formal and excessive, especially for young people. Youth is inclined to exaggerate its sufferings, especially those caused by failures in love. Still, it is conceivable that these young people might be too much in love with being in love, and that this obsession may influence their language. Perhaps their inflated speech should not be taken at face value. If this is true, then their language requires a sense of internal plausibility to reinforce the humorous irony.

Sometimes, the very utterance of Shakespeare's language becomes too rhetorical for a satisfactory modern performance. *A Midsummer Night's Dream* has been quoted so often and so automatically that it has no want of language traps. Frequently, the language spoken on stage sounds so far removed from the modern ear that it seems better suited to a museum or classroom. This is usually the result of too much dependence on the rhetorical features of the language – its syntax, metrics, and versification – and too little attention to the meaning. If only the actor can find the rhetorical clues in the language, some experts say, Shakespeare's language thereby teaches the actor how to perform his plays. Actually, Shakespeare's language is a combination of rhetoric *and* dramatic action, a partnership that significantly colours its utterance and ensures that it remains continuously fresh and entertaining in performance. In all probability, the overly rhetorical type of utterance found in some performances does not come from the language as such, but mainly from the absence of a fully developed interpretation.

Psychologically speaking, Shakespeare's comedies are often thought to be among the most trouble-free classic plays to deal with, while the plays of Henrik Ibsen, Anton Chekhov, or Eugene O'Neill are among the most complex. It is said that Shakespeare merely involves 'role-play' and 'period style', while Ibsen, Chekhov and O'Neill, for example, involve psychological depth and complexity. In terms of internal plausibility, however, *Midsummer* presents some very difficult challenges indeed. The place to look for this elusive internal plausibility is in the dense clusters of psychology ('units' or 'pieces' in Stanislavsky's lexicon) that are omnipresent in the lovers' language (and elsewhere in *Midsummer* too). In these linguistic clusters, the motives of Shakespeare's characters reveal themselves as more complex than in many intentionally psychological plays. Since this fact is not always immediately obvious, to notice it will require careful, even obsessive attention to the text. Directors who value textual precision and do not recoil from textual complexity will find a useful ally in Active Analysis. Farther ahead, it will be shown that Active Analysis depends for its effectiveness on precisely this kind of detailed, text-based mindfulness.

FURTHER THOUGHTS

Ever since Freud and Stanislavsky, the question of internal plausibility has been of paramount importance in play production. For plays that follow the customary norms of lifelike time, place and action, the question is usually not that of plausibility as such, but more often that of insight and complexity. For plays that do not follow such norms, however, the question of internal plausibility in the exact sense of the term forces itself on the attention of the director. This question is most noticeable in a play's treatment of time, place and action. In the first part of this book, attention tends to be focused on the internal plausibility of the action. But what about the internal plausibility of time and place?

How is the passage of time treated in the play? In *Midsummer*, time seems to pass continuously, in realistic fashion, from the beginning of the play to its end. Unfortunately, as many commentators have pointed out, this impression does not always coincide with the actual passage of time in the play. Technically, it should transpire over the course of five days, including the final day of the wedding, but only three days are accounted for in the action. A time warp seems to occur once the action reaches the forest. Is this something that should be made prominent in production, or should it, as some have said, be overlooked simply as an authorial irregularity?

How is place treated in the play? Theseus's palace and Quince's house are plausibly identifiable locales, but after the action reaches the forest, the locales tend to become somewhat unclear. There could be as little as two or as many as four separate locales in the forest, depending on one's reading of the text. What is the internal plausibility for the possibility of two forest locales? Three? Four? Where are these locales in relation to each other geographically? Does the action proceed from one forest locale to another in an internally plausible manner? If not, should this factor be made prominent in performance or is it another irregularity in the writing?

Clichés

In Shakespeare's plays particularly, there are the inevitable clichés of characterization to be on guard against. How do dukes and duchesses, kings and queens, young lovers, labourers and fairies and elves behave? Pictures instantly appear in one's imagination: royalty is always stately and aristocratic; young lovers are handsome and attractive, and generally vacuous; labourers are foolish and clumsy; and fairies and elves resemble those portrayed in early Walt Disney films. Some analysts feel that since these images have become fixed over the years, directors should simply accept them. To do otherwise, they say, is just plain egotism. Of course, there are egotists in every line of creative work, not only in directing. Moreover, a non-traditional interpretation is not always a genuine innovation either. On the other hand, creativity begins precisely at those points where a director senses the possibility of something conventional or worn out in a play. Most directors would like their productions to add something fresh to what has already been done. What if Puck is reminiscent of Caliban, Godzilla, a teenager on a skateboard, or a white rabbit? Most directors tend to avoid extremes, but the time is probably over when Puck resembles Peter Pan or Tinker Bell. The remarkable success of Pixar films in the last decade owes much to its fresh, contemporary mode of thinking; Active Analysis promotes a similarly contemporary mode of thinking for the stage.

The Mechanicals. Except for the biased opinions of Puck and Philostrate, nothing in the text actually specifies that all these characters need to be foolish and clumsy. Directors may recognize this as a likely cliché. The conversation between Titania and Bottom catches one's attention again in this respect. The episode immediately pictures itself: Titania awakes, runs to the ass, embraces him, and utters some stylish poetry about love. Why meddle with it? Because a complex cluster of psychology is actually present there, though the episode needs to be closely analyzed to reveal this and avoid it becoming a cliché. Active Analysis promotes the singular skills necessary for identifying such 'not immediately obvious' instances in the text and for finding fresh, contemporary, internally plausible motivations to support them.

FURTHER THOUGHTS

Clichés tend to arrive uninvited when we try to describe characters. Thus, the first step in avoiding clichés is the language we use. It is difficult to describe potentially stereotypical characters without resorting to words and phrases heard frequently in everyday conversation, newscasts, advertising and literature classes. Yet the effort to avoid clichés in one's own language is one of the major responsibilities of the modern director. It is said that Jerzy Grotowski made a conscious effort to refresh his artistic vocabulary after every production.

The behaviour of the royal figures in the play was evaluated above somewhat lightly. In fact, their behaviour often exposes some of the most obvious clichés in productions of this play. In *Midsummer*, there are episodes of private as well as public behaviour of royalty. How does 'royalty' behave in these differing situations? After all, royalty are human beings before they are royalty. Moreover, each royal figure in *Midsummer* has his/her own given circumstances. Theseus is a warrior, philanderer and Duke of Athens. Hippolyta is a warrior, lesbian, and Queen of Amazonia. Even more challenging is the behaviour of the fairy royalty. Oberon is a fairy, a warrior and a king. Titania is a fairy and a queen. According to stage tradition, royalty is usually performed by tall, attractive men and women behaving in a self-consciously well-mannered fashion. Nevertheless, how do these figures really 'behave'?

Genre

Genre is a particular relation to and point of view toward the world, which serves as a norm or set of expectations to guide our experience of a play. Genre provides a sense of how and why things happen the way they do in a play and in this capacity, it guides the overall understanding and execution of a production.

Since every genre depends on a set of assumptions, the director working with Active Analysis therefore needs to present a starting point, even if subsequent homework and rehearsal might lead to changing it. Certainly, directors could put an end to this question by simply allowing literary critics to make the decision for them. *Midsummer* has been classified variously as a comedy, romance, fantasy, comic drama, romantic comedy and even a dark satire. It would seem that all a director needs to do is select an agreeable classification, consider the relevant information, and apply it to the play. According to the thinking that underlies Active Analysis, the director's determination of a play's genre is a much more complex and personal matter than this. For that reason, additional time needs to be given to this concept, since a proper understanding of genre is important for not only *Midsummer* but also later on, when it will guide Active Analysis rehearsals as well.

To understand a play's genre, it is important to know its author well. We will be looking for facts in Shakespeare's life that could shed some light on the play's basic subject, which we will identify for the moment as 'love.' With Active Analysis, study of the author's life begins from a fact from *inside the play*, namely love, rather than from outside, viz. literary theories and issues of identity politics, gender studies, economics, philosophy, myth and archetype, etc.

We know that Shakespeare's marriage to Anne Hathaway was complex. She was seven years older than he was, and the age difference, plus the fact that she was already pregnant with their first child when they married in 1582, could be a sign that marriage was pressed on a hesitant groom. There is also some mention of another woman in Shakespeare's life at the time, whose existence may have pressed the Hathaway family to have their daughter married before Shakespeare changed his mind. The marriage banns were announced only once rather than the traditional three times. Some scholars believe that Shakespeare's dislike of Anne Hathaway was a factor in his decision to quit Stratford around 1585 for London, where he remained for the next twenty-five years, leaving his wife and children behind. Of added significance is the fact that in his will Shakespeare bequeathed to Anne Hathaway his 'second-best bed'.

Shakespeare researchers have provided other explanations for these facts. All the same, it is plausible to assume that from an early age Shakespeare had a shrewd awareness of *the realities of love.*

In aid of genre, it is also necessary to become familiar with the author's other works. Something might be discoverable in them that helps to understand the present play. In *As You Like It,* Rosalind laughs at Orlando's love poems, in which he sentimentalizes, or fetishizes, women ('. . . men have died from time to time, and worms have eaten them, but not for love.' [4.1.80–81]). In *Twelfth Night,* Orsino is delighted by the fact that his love for Olivia makes him feel unwell ('If music be the food of love, play on; / Give me excess of it, that, surfeiting, / The appetite may sicken, and so die.' [1.1.1–3]). He too fetishizes women. An ironic attitude toward love appears throughout *Much Ado About Nothing,* as when Benedick overstates his disapproval of Claudio's romantic love for Hero, an action that involuntarily exposes Benedick's unacknowledged love for Beatrice ('Shall I never see a bachelor of three-score again? / Go to, i' faith; an thou wilt needs thrust thy neck / into a yoke, wear the print of it and sigh away / Sundays.' [1.1.179–182]). *Love's Labours Lost,* written about the same time as *Midsummer,* satirizes the masculine inclination to fetishize women as tempting love objects instead of as individuals ('If any man be seen to talk with a woman / within the term of three years, he shall endure such / public shame as the rest of the court can possibly devise.' [1.1.134–136]).

That Shakespeare was alert to inflated expressions of love can also be seen in his Sonnet 130 ('My mistress' eyes are nothing like the sun . . .').This sonnet echoes the extravagantly poetic conversation between Hermia and Lysander when they are alone together after hearing the Duke's command for her to obey her father's will (1.1.136–149). And these passages echo the expression of fetishistic love between Romeo and Juliet when they first meet at the ball (1.5.93–106).

In these selections and others, Shakespeare's characters express *their love* with resolute earnestness and without any explicit acknowledgement of what *our attitude* toward the subject is meant to be. Since elaborately worked language is standard with Shakespeare, even special attention given to this issue in production is no guarantee that potentially ironic meaning will be successfully conveyed to the audience. How is a director to detect whether the extracts mentioned above are meant to have double meanings? Shakespeare's elaborate language can only be effective to the degree that what it aims to express is actually recognized as being deliberately intended. In other words, irony can only be effective for those who understand the attitude being expressed and therefore the point of the irony. This is one reason why much of Shakespeare's irony is so easily missed.

Reading *Midsummer* again, particular interest arises from a passage that was already looked at, but without sufficiently considering its meaning:

> HIPPOLYTA. But all the story of the night told over,
>   And *all their minds transfigur'd so together,*
>   *More witnesseth than fancy's images,*
>   *And grows to something of great constancy*;
>   But howsoever strange and admirable. (5.1.23–27, italics added)

Hippolyta suspects there is 'something of great constancy' in the young lovers' misadventures in the woods. Their stories tend to agree with each other, which makes her suspect they share a meaning that is not immediately obvious, at least to Oberon. This thought brings to mind something T. S. Eliot said about *A Midsummer Night's Dream*:

> In some of [Shakespeare's] sophisticated comedies, what has been crude 'comic relief' is more nearly 'taken up to a higher unity of feeling.' In *A Midsummer Night's Dream* the farcical element is an essential to a pattern more complex and elaborate than any constructed by a dramatist before or since.[2]

Eliot's words about 'a higher unity of feeling' echo those of Hippolyta.

Bearing in mind Hippolyta's observation, Eliot's statement, and certain patterns of love detected in Shakespeare's life and works, perhaps we can begin to understand more of what is in *Midsummer*. In the search for an appropriate genre to guide our experience of the play, the viewpoint of a 'fable' begins to emerge as a strong possibility. A fable is a story that purposefully expresses a moral meaning, often gives human qualities to mythological and non-human subjects, and contains supernatural or exaggerated natural incidents. Examples are Aesop's *Fables*, George Orwell's *Animal Farm*, and *Gulliver's Travels* by Jonathan Swift, and significantly, the plays of Bertolt Brecht. In fables, characters are not only understood as human figures but also as representatives of particular values or ways of thinking about the world. The conventions of fable now shift our attention from the often-ridiculous behaviour of the characters in *Midsummer* to the worldview that is their controlling impulse. With this distinctive awareness, we can begin to understand that the unexpected behaviours, extraordinary incidents, and even the supernatural characters in *Midsummer* comprise not only a Shakespearean love story but also a fable, a 'romantic fable', that is, a romantic comedy with a moral meaning. Future work with the various phases of Active Analysis is now better defined because it can be encompassed within the conventions of a romantic fable.

FURTHER THOUGHTS

A genre may be understood theoretically as well as personally. The director who wishes to work with Active Analysis ought to establish both understandings as starting points before attempting to describe the genre of the play with which he/she is currently occupied. As an exercise, compare the director's personal definitions of comedy, romance, fantasy, comic drama, romantic comedy and satire with their academic definitions. It will likely be found that there are as many personal definitions of these genres among directors as there are theoretical definitions among scholars. Moreover, for directors there is also the question of how to express comedy, romance, fantasy, comic drama, romantic comedy and satire in the acting, direction and design. In the final analysis, both the academic definitions and the personal understandings of genre are points of view toward the life and the world. This is the understanding of genre with which the director ought to come to terms, particularly as someone who wishes to take the fullest possible advantage of Active Analysis.

3

Director's Plan: Action Analysis

Having considered the most obvious of the general challenges, it is now time for a more detailed study of the play itself. The methodology of this process is of vital importance in Active Analysis and comprises two parts: the requirements of the actor and director, and the additional requirements of the director. The first part was codified by Maria Knebel based on her work with Stanislavsky in his final years. We have adapted this process and called it Action Analysis. The director draws on its results for use in 'around-the-table' rehearsals and throughout Active Analysis rehearsals. The second part we have called Formalist Analysis, and it comprises a greatly expanded version of the first. This part can be equally valuable for actors, but customarily, if not regrettably, its potentials are given over almost exclusively to directors. Whatever happens, both parts of this detailed study are inseparably linked and equally necessary for the director who wishes to work with Active Analysis. Readers may find a comprehensive treatment of these processes in my book, *Script Analysis for Actors, Directors, and Designers*. For our purposes here, it is only necessary to provide an abbreviated version of Action Analysis. The point is that the conventions, vocabulary and outcomes of Action Analysis provide the primary means of communication between director and actors in the rehearsal phase of Active Analysis to come.

(Some features of Action Analysis are likely to be familiar for directors who are already acquainted with Stanislavsky's system. Although he devised and explained them in his writings, of course, nevertheless later writers and directors, including myself, have adopted and adapted them with improved clarity and conciseness for modern use.)

Exercise: Reading Stanislavsky unabridged

For over half a century, the standard English-language texts of Stanislavsky have been those translated by Elizabeth R. Hapgood (*An Actor Prepares,* 1936; *Building a Character,* 1949; and *Creating a Role,* 1961). Unfortunately, the Russian originals these translations were based upon were themselves written in haste by Stanislavsky and, in the case of the third book, merely collected by editors from random assortments of his unpublished notes. Valuable as these initial translations have been, by common consent they have always been considered inadequate to the task, owing to a combination of hasty composition, Soviet censorship and editorial idiosyncrasies. Fortunately, the new translations by Jean Benedetti, in partnership with Anatoly Smeliansky (Russia's foremost Stanislavsky authority), have successfully addressed these inadequacies by providing comprehensive, authoritative and readable new translations (*An Actor's Work: A Student's Diary,* 2008; *An Actor's Work on a Role,* 2009). Since Active Analysis is based on Stanislavsky's system of acting, it is understood that directors wishing to employ this process will be familiar with those principles. Not only through hearsay, but mainly through practice and a working knowledge of the latest translations of Stanislavsky's own words on the subject.

Thinking eventfully

By design, the chief feature of play analysis and rehearsal practice for Active Analysis is also the easiest and most accessible way to come to terms with a play, any play: the events of the plot. The term 'event' as it is used here does not refer to anything that happens, but only to those that normally would not or should not happen: unexpected arrivals or departures, discoveries, misunderstandings or misidentifications, breaches of social norms, accidents of nature, and so on. Such events are always first time or last time occurrences in a play. In this technical sense, events change something, bring about new ideas and feelings in the characters, or force characters to see life in a new way and consequently change the direction of their path in the play.

Events are sometimes thought of as turning points or climaxes, and, just as there are major and minor turning points and climaxes, so too there are major and minor events. Since plays are usually obliged to uphold a time limit of two-three hours, the number of major events, major turning points and climaxes, must by necessity be limited to some degree. Active Analysis obliges the director to identify these major events and provide them with vivid titles that describe – and this point is essential – the associated 'framing event'. A framing event is that which governs the external events and without which the external events would not exist qua events. For example, the external event taking place at this moment between you, the reader, and me, the author, is 'reading a book about Active Analysis', something that is taking place physically in the here and now; really and solidly, not abstractly. Whereas the associated framing event (depending on the surrounding circumstances, of course) might be 'seeking advice from an expert' (Stanislavsky), 'ignoring someone' (by pretending to read), 'making a fresh start', 'cramming for an exam', or even 'impressing the teacher'. In other words, a framing event is the abstracted essence of an external event considered together with the surrounding circumstances. Concise, memorable titles like these examples are important because external events and their associated framing events will be repeatedly tested, refined and adjusted during the rehearsal phase of Active Analysis. Events in this technical sense are the director's principal means of communication with the actors in Active Analysis.

Exercise

Imagine that a husband and wife have quarrelled about the value of an abstract painting and then go to a police station to have a report drawn up. The police officer, having established that no physical assault, use of force, or any other offence against civil or criminal law has taken place, refuses to write up a report in view of the lack of an event. From his point of view, nothing has happened. For a psychologist, moralist, social scientist, or art historian, however, the incident referred to is indeed an event. In other words, the same event represents something crucial from one point of view, something meaningless from another, and from yet another it does not exist.

To understand this idea more clearly, Stanislavsky suggested looking back on one's own life and trying to remember a significant event in order to understand how it influenced our later relations with others. Of course, it is easy to identify such events in one's own life. But now try to appreciate the significance of an event not for oneself but for someone else, and notice how mistaken we can be in our estimate of an event from their point of view. Even for that of a close friend or relative, it is not an easy task. Empathy – the capacity to recognize or understand another's state of mind or emotion – is essential to appreciate what is significant in someone else's life. To do so effectively, it would be necessary to study all the circumstances that predetermined the given event, all the motives that led the other person to perform this or that action. It would probably be necessary to interview the person and obtain some very personal information for such a purpose.

Chain of external events

Of the four plots in *Midsummer*, we will concentrate on the plight of the young lovers, which is usually considered the main plot of the play. Obviously, each of the other plots requires an analysis of its own, but for practical purposes, those analyses would employ much the same process.

With Active Analysis, events are described in terms of reciprocal actions that take place before our eyes, on stage, in the here and now. As in, X does to Y and Y does to X. Events are always specific, concrete, and in some way actable.

1   External Event: Egeus demands that Theseus must validate his paternal rights, and Theseus stalls Egeus for time. Title of

Framing Event: 'A hysterical father makes an irrational demand.'

2   External Event: Hermia warns Lysander about the perils of their situation, and Lysander reassures Hermia about their safety. Title of Framing Event: 'Criminals on the run from the law.'

3   External Event: Helena pleads for Demetrius's love and Demetrius warns Helena against her reckless behaviour. Title: 'Dangerously obsessive love.'

4   External Event: Theseus orders Puck to reform 'rash' Demetrius by means of the magic nectar, and Puck eagerly consents to Theseus's order. Title of Framing Event: 'A mischievous plan.'

5   External Event: Puck mistakenly enchants Lysander, and sleeping Lysander takes no notice of Puck. Title of Framing Event: 'A risky magic spell.'

6   External Event: Demetrius and Lysander simultaneously plead for Helena's love, and Helena scolds Demetrius and Lysander for making fun of her for being 'unlovable'. Title of Framing Event: 'Two men demand to love the same woman.'

7   External Event: Helena blames Hermia for conspiring with Demetrius and Lysander against her, and Hermia faults Helena for a spiteful practical joke. Title of Framing Event: 'A mutual misunderstanding among friends.'

8   External Event: Lysander challenges Demetrius to a duel, and Demetrius accepts Lysander's challenge. Title: 'An affair of honour.'

9   External Event: Theseus orders Lysander and Demetrius to explain what has happened, and Lysander and Demetrius express regret to Theseus. Title of Framing Event: 'An embarrassing apology.'

10 External Event: Egeus reminds Theseus of his promise, and Theseus overrules Egeus. Title of Framing Event: 'A judicial verdict reversed.'

There may be differences of opinion about the particulars of these accounts, but the logic behind them should be clear enough for illustrative purposes. This chain of external events will be consulted in rehearsal during a process of controlled improvisations and testing called 'etudes'. There will be more information about etudes when we enter the rehearsal phase of the director's work. But for the moment, Action Analysis needs to continue.

Exercise

Determine the Chain of External Events and their titles for the secondary plot lines:

- Theseus and Hippolyta

- The Mechanicals

- Oberon and Titania

First, try to do this independently, and then as a group. What specific difficulties are encountered in attempting to carry out this exercise both independently and as a group? Did any special difficulties arise when trying to pinpoint a governing title for each event? Where do the events of one plot line intersect with those of another? What are the causes and effects of these comings together?

Seed

Another component of Action Analysis that is essential for Active Analysis is that of the play's 'seed', or basic subject, which consists of a special pattern of action underlying the chain of external events. (This extremely useful concept was named and devised by Nemirovich-Danchenko and subsequently introduced into Stanislavsky's own thinking as well.) A seed in nature is a source of development or growth, and the seed of a play is the source of its development and growth as a creative work. Today we might think of this as the play's DNA, because it contains the 'genetic instructions' for the development and operation of every part of the play. The seed of *Midsummer* can be readily identified as love, although it also has a special Shakespearean quality, which we might call '*romantic* love', or less politely, 'fetishistic love'. Here then we have a provisional statement of the basic subject that directly or indirectly influences all the events in the play and toward which all the characters express a unique disposition. It is still provisional at this point because it has not been tested to confirm that it accurately adheres to the definition of a seed.

Incidentally, the seed of director Max Reinhardt's production (1927) and later film (1935) was 'romantic fun'. That of Peter Brook's famous 1970 production was 'joyful sex'. In addition, according to critic Jan Kott's influential book (*Shakespeare Our Contemporary*, 1964), the basic subject of *Midsummer* is 'animalistic sex'. These instances show how a director's perception of the seed can be both accurate according to the play itself as well as a reflection or even a well-thought-out distortion (cf. 'romantic fun' in the midst of the Great Depression) of one's own time and culture as well.

Exercise

Vladimir Nemirovich-Danchenko visited Hollywood in 1926–1927 in an effort to study and perhaps have some influence on the then-emergent American film industry. A learning moment about the concept of the seed occurred when he was asked to participate in the planning for a film of Tolstoy's novel, *Anna Karenina*, which was ultimately released in 1935 (directed by Clarence Brown with Greta Garbo in the leading role). Since Nemirovich was in the process of adapting and directing a stage version for the Moscow Art Theatre (1937), his thoughts were thought to be potentially helpful for the producers of the Hollywood film. For Hollywood, the seed of the novel was 'motherhood'. Hence, Anna commits suicide because of her professed failure as a mother. Nemirovich strongly disagreed. He recognized that the basic subject was not motherhood, but 'passion', which, of course, the Hollywood producers refused to accept on moral grounds.

Consider the difference between these two versions of the novel's seed. Turning to the present, consider recent films, novels, or plays from the point of view of the seed. Can it be recognized how the seed governs the entire work? At which points in the work does the seed reveal itself most noticeably? Least noticeably? Are there episodes in the work where the seed is genuinely absent? Are there possible justifications for such an absence?

Chain of internal events

Testing the provisional seed is accomplished by determining if it is genuinely present within each external event, and if so, in what manner. That romantic love is the seed of *Midsummer* would seem to be an obvious fact. All the same, testing is necessary not only to confirm the seed's identity and accuracy but also to understand and show how it emerges through the actions of the characters. The following chain of internal events follows the numbering of the earlier chain of external events, and the seed here is italicized.

1 Internal Event: Egeus denounces *romantic love*.

2 Internal Event: Hermia and Lysander discover the dangers of *romantic love*.

3 Internal Event: *Romantic love* sets off a conflict between Helena and Demetrius.

4 Internal Event: Oberon plans to restore *romantic love* for Helena in Demetrius's heart.

5 Internal Event: Puck mishandles the *romantic love* nectar.

6 Internal Event: Demetrius and Lysander become unsuspecting victims of misdirected *romantic love*.

7 Internal Event: Misdirected *romantic love* obliges Hermia and Helena to end their friendship.

8 Internal Event: Misdirected *romantic love* obliges Lysander and Demetrius to challenge each other to a duel.

9 Internal Event: The improbabilities of *romantic love* bewilder Lysander and Demetrius.

10 Internal Event: Theseus officially authorizes *romantic love.*

Exposing how consistently romantic love operates both in the text and subtext of *Midsummer* shows it to be an accurate formulation of the seed.

Exercise

Determine the chain of internal events for one of the secondary plots. For example, the plot comprising Oberon and Titania. How could their custody battle possibly be related to romantic love? The clue lies in the fact that they were once in love romantically, but now they are married. Hence, Shakespeare has provided a portrait of romantic love *after the fact.* Notice that the presence and functionality of the seed in this plot is ironic and therefore more challenging to trace than in the main plot of the young lovers, where it is a direct outcome of their actions. In such circumstances it is particularly important to maintain one's faith in the concept and value of the seed, and so to exercise relentless determination in seeking out its minutest operations. Sometimes the presence of the seed may give the impression of being unduly microscopic, but by definition, the seed is nonetheless crucial to the artistic unity of the play, whereby all its elements cooperate to accomplish its main purpose.

Theme

Readers can probably think of many plays that share this seed, the basic subject of romantic love. What ultimately distinguishes all such plays is their theme, their approach to the seed, their individual attitudes toward the basic subject. Consider, for example, the differing attitudes toward romantic love expressed in *Romeo and Juliet, Much Ado About Nothing, The Taming of the Shrew, Love's Labours Lost* or *As You Like It.* Romantic love is clearly present in all these plays, but it is experienced quite differently in each one. That is to say, their seeds may be identical, but their themes are not. For *Midsummer*, Lysander directly states the theme the first time he and Hermia are alone together. (Incidentally, direct statement of theme is a distinctive feature of the genre of fable.) Not suprisingly, he states it in the form of a proverb he has often found in his readings of 'tale or history': 'The course of true love never did run smooth.' It is true, of course, that love never runs smoothly in all the plays mentioned above, but only in *Midsummer* is this proverb specifically the theme, or main idea of the play. Returning our attention to Action Analysis, the theme allows us to recognize each event as part of a coherent point of view toward romantic love.

Exercise

Returning once again to the secondary plots, try to determine the specific attitude toward romantic love expressed in each one. The very purpose of a secondary plot is to foreground different *facets* of the main plot, not to repeat it. Accordingly, it will be noticed that the themes of the secondary plots are not exactly the same as that of the main plot. Otherwise, the play would be dramaturgically repetitious. As a result, it is important to determine the 'sub-themes' expressed by each of these secondary plot lines. By definition, the stories of Theseus and Hippolyta, the Mechanicals, and Oberon and Titania ought to be manifest variations of the proverb, 'The course of true love never did run smooth'. What exactly happens in these secondary plots that is related to but different from what happens in the main plot involving the young lovers?

Beginning, middle, end

Like any work of art, a play must have a finished form. In narrative works such as drama, fiction and film, finished form is identified by the presence of a beginning, middle and end. For stage directors, this concept is usually understood in structural terms as the three major climaxes of a play. In Stanislavsky's work, this concept emerged as the 'perspective of a role', which is much the same idea, only from an actor's point of view. For Michael Chekhov, awareness of the beginning, middle and end is an explicit feature of his approach to acting. Here are suggestions for the beginning, middle and end of *Midsummer*:

- Beginning: Egeus demands that Theseus endorse his paternal rights. This event is technically the first major climax, also identified as the 'inciting action'.

- Middle: Lysander and Demetrius challenge each other to a duel. This event is technically the second major climax. After this turning point, Oberon's manoeuverings tend to control the action.

- End: Theseus overrules Egeus's demand. This event is technically the third major climax. The following scene between Theseus and Hippolyta is a clarification of its meaning. The final scene is technically an epilogue, which is a condensed restatement of the play's action and meaning.

In Active Analysis, the director uses the concepts of beginning, middle, and end as a means for guiding the actors toward an awareness of each episode's function in the overall production. This awareness is also implicit in the time-honoured performance axiom, 'Do not play the end at the beginning!'

Exercise

Compare the beginning, middle and end of the main plot with those same features in each of the secondary plots. Besides revealing the 'sub-themes' with more clarity, what other features of the play begin to emerge that may have been less immediately obvious before this? Amidst other advantages, this exercise can also help to expose latent details in the characters' relationships.

Through-action and counter through-action

The seed and theme are, of course, intellectual concepts. This awareness is what led Stanislavsky to develop the 'through-action' as a device to explain how these intellectual concepts operate in psychophysical terms, on stage, before our eyes. His device consists of a concise *actable* formulation of the play's main plot.[1] Every character possesses a through-action, certainly, but that of the main character defines the essence of the whole play, and logically why he/she is called the 'main character'.

What kind of thinking is needed to identify the through-action? As we stated earlier, the main plot of *Midsummer* is that of Lysander and Hermia, and the controlling figure of this plot is Lysander. Technically speaking, this makes Lysander the protagonist, or main character, of the play, though the other plots tend to obscure this fact in performance. Lysander is in love with Hermia, of course, but in a larger sense, he is battling against all the enemies of romantic love. He is a 'political activist' in his commitment to the belief that 'Love conquers all things'. For that reason, a plausible formulation of his through-action would be, 'A romantic young "knight" protects a "persecuted maiden" and defends her from the murderous intentions of her "evil father".' (Theseus authorizes the legal consequences, but it is Egeus who provokes him to do so.) As the protagonist, Lysander also carries the meaning of the entire play on his shoulders, so to speak. His through-action governs the play through its secondary plots, which are fun-house mirror reflections of his battle against the enemies of love. These reflections form the 'facets' of romantic love referred to earlier.

Where the protagonist is the subject of the through-action, it is logical that the antagonist will be the subject of the counter-through-action. With the exception of different subjects and actions, the formal requirements of the counter-through-action are identical to those of the through-action. Although Egeus takes part in only two scenes (three, if he appears in the final scene, which sometimes happens in performance), nevertheless he is still the major force working against Lysander throughout the play. His through-action may be formulated in this way: 'A protective father challenges a deceitful suitor over control of his naïve daughter's fate.' This formulation is from Egeus's point of view, of course. To repeat, neither of these formulations ought to be taken as authoritative, but merely as illustrations of the thinking processes involved in formulating the through-action and counter through-action.

Exercise

In one of the secondary plots, Theseus is the protagonist and Hippolyta is the antagonist. In another, Bottom is the protagonist and Quince the antagonist. In the third, Oberon is the protagonist and Titania the antagonist. With this information in mind, formulate the through-action and counter through-action for each secondary plot line. Compare the results. Can it be recognized how each secondary plot is a 'fun-house mirror reflection' of the plight of the young lovers?

4

An Introductory Conversation with Stanislavsky about Active Analysis

Before moving on to rehearsals with the actors, it will be helpful to obtain an idea of the philosophy and practice of Active Analysis in its earliest usage. We can do no better for this task than consult the original words of Stanislavsky in conversation with a director for whom Active Analysis was an exciting, if puzzling, departure from his mentor's well-known original earlier practice.

As stated earlier, Stanislavsky did not have the opportunity to write down all his ideas about Active Analysis in an organized form. (Nor did he ever assign this title to it. That was done later by Maria Knebel.) Nevertheless, he continued to develop this process with students at his home-studio. With particularly gifted students, such as Knebel, he made a special effort to explain the basic principles behind his evolving method. Another such gifted student was the St Petersburg actor and director, Boris Zon (1898–1966), who visited Stanislavsky during the later years of his life. Zon was also a teacher at the Leningrad (now St Petersburg) Theatre Institute and founder of the Leningrad Theatre for Young Audiences.[1] Though not very well known in Russia even today, Zon was nevertheless a major inspiration in the careers of many prominent Russian actors and directors. One of those inspired by Zon was Oleg Yefremov (1927–2000), one of Russia's finest and most influential actors and directors, and Artistic

Director of the Moscow Art Theatre (1970–2000) at a time that witnessed the rebirth of MAT after a long period of Soviet restrictions. Zon, said Yefremov, was 'one of the last and maybe the brightest pupils of Stanislavsky'.[2]

Zon had heard about the experimental rehearsal method Stanislavsky was developing at the time and in April 1933, he made a special trip to Moscow to learn more about it, hoping to talk with Stanislavsky himself. A collection of Zon's writings was recently published in Russia, and here is an informative passage about this emergent process from his memoirs:

Rehearsal ended. I stood up to leave with everyone else, but Stanislavsky drew me by the hand and we sat down on the sofa together. He looked tired and did not smile; in his eyes, I saw a question: 'Well, what do you think? Tell me.' Despite a great temptation to remain with Stanislavsky, a chance I had never dreamed of, I was reluctant to begin the conversation.

'Aren't you tired, Konstantin Sergeyevich?'

'It's nothing. I can never rest right after a rehearsal. I need to get away from it for a while. Speak up. What is clear, what is not? I do not know how prepared you are, and after all, everything cannot be explained at one go . . .'

I was so filled by all I had seen and heard that my eyes literally teared up. Hundreds of questions boiled up in my mind, and I did not know which ones to grasp. First, I spoke about how many times I had seen him and his work on stage in the past. [I also said that] I had repeatedly read *My Life in Art* and was familiar with everything written about it and about the Moscow Art Theatre. But now, for the first time, I was seeing him up close and observing his creative process.

'So, what did they write?' he asked.

I had to admit that at that moment all my ideas about the 'Stanislavsky System' had been so strongly shaken that even today I cannot describe to what degree. And this in spite of the fact that several years before [this meeting] I had the good fortune [. . .] to take a two-year course of study in Moscow about his system, with his approval, from a student of Evgeny Vakhtangov.[3]

'That is good,' Stanislavsky said. 'But unfortunately, Vakhtangov died long ago, and eleven years have passed. And during these years we have had to rethink a lot of things, and give up much that seemed indisputable to us earlier.'

'So now I have a feeling,' I confessed, 'that until today I have been blind and suddenly I can see clearly. Everything I knew so well actually looks so differently now that it needs to be learned all over again.'

'So ask,' Konstantin Sergeyevich offered.

And I began to ask questions.

Question: How long do you work at the table now, and when do you go to the next stage?

Answer: Today we read the play, tomorrow – we act. If it is not enough to read the play once, we will read it again.

Question: Even though the actors know nothing yet?

Answer: They do not know the words, but they know what to do. If they forget, I will remind them. If a question arises, we will look at the text: 'Excuse me, but the text seems to say something about that in the third act. Let's look for it,' etc.

Question: So, you do not need the text of the roles at first?

Answer: We will approach it step by step. The only logical way is through action.

Question: In other words, you do not sit at the table at all?

Answer: They can sit anywhere . . . The actors can always sit 'at the table' for new attempts as they come up.

Question: What new works have you done using this method?

Answer: Completely, still only one. Partially, in all our latest work. The fact is that over-reliance on table work led us to 'indigestion'. Like a capon fed on so many nuts that its stomach no longer digests any food, so too the actor is preconditioned with so much 'food' at the table that he cannot reproduce it immediately, cannot use one-hundredth of what was accumulated. My new method is a development of our previous work.

Question: As far as I understood from today's rehearsal, you lead the actor to an involuntary emergence of characterization through the process of action – and all this comes from the actor himself?

Answer: Certainly.

Question: And how do the character's features develop – age, profession, nationality, and so forth?

Answer: Only from the action. For example, an old man . . . What prevents him from moving quickly? His heart, his legs. Find special etudes for the heart and 'wooden' legs. If necessary, tie up the legs with a towel around the knees. Feel what interferes with movement. I am explaining this very primitively, but the process is essentially the same in all cases.

Question: When and how are pieces [units] and tasks [objectives] established now?

Answer: As I said, we work with a kind of 'secret' plan. We watch the acting, and when it appears that the actors have played one piece [unit], then a new one begins. We played, for example, 'a meeting', and now, presumably, we are playing 'an acquaintance'. The task [objective] arises spontaneously of its own accord. What is important is that [finding] the task is easy. Maybe it is accurate, maybe not. We reach for something else, go on to the next action, and play it.

Question: How do you achieve relaxation of the muscles?[4]

Answer: By proceeding from nature in everything and ultimately forgetting about 'theatre'. Generally speaking, there is no system, there is only nature. And my entire life I have attempted to come as close as possible to it. You asked about relaxation of the muscles. Why is simply walking on stage so difficult to do? Because we are embarrassed on stage, embarrassed from false traditions and from bad taste that spoils our natures.

Question: Does it follow from your theatrical principles that the director should be cautious with his expressive means, and that the designer – I am talking about production values – is given a very modest place?

Answer: I welcome the most sophisticated and complex production values when they are justified through the actor. But since scenic design is still at an extraordinary low level,[5] and since actors still lack the kind of elementary literacy that painters and musicians have – we dare not force the actors to do things that are beyond their [present] abilities. There would still be no truthfulness in it. And the virtuosity of the director or the designer has nothing to do with the art of the theatre.[6]

The experience of the 1905 studio, [Stanislavsky continued,] where Meyerhold and I (neither of us wealthy people) worked together for the first time, wasted large amounts of money.[7] I am absolutely convinced of it. I wasted money, but that did not enable the plays to return the spent money to me, of course, although it did delay for many years the development of Russian theatre.

Konstantin Sergeyevich looked at my notebook, which I kept with me all four hours of rehearsal and where I continue to write everything down even now.

'I do not recognize any secrets in art,' he said, 'and I would like others to take as much as possible from my experience, but not a single line of my book can be published yet.'

I hastened to assure him that I write only for myself, for my practical work with actors and students, and not to print or reveal to journalists anything I am collecting.

'To the actors and students, please . . . tell, explain, and try. And then be sure to tell me what turns out. This is terribly important for me,' Stanislavsky added seriously. 'And what you have written down, show me that, too. I want to know how all of you understand this . . .'

With this conversation, my first meeting with Konstantin Sergeyevich came to an end. After receiving an invitation from him to attend tomorrow's rehearsal, I felt immensely rich, inspired, happy, and I rushed off to examine my rough notes.[8]

5

Active Analysis in Rehearsal

The homework phase of Active Analysis is ended for the time being, and now the moment has arrived when the director assembles the performers and begins the process of Active Analysis in rehearsal. This is done by a reciprocal process of table work and etudes, which will be treated next. However, since Active Analysis is likely to be a new experience for the actors (as it was for Zon), the director needs to handle its introduction to the actors very carefully. Active Analysis is a long and difficult process. For most of the actors, it will not only be a new way of rehearsing but also the first time they have read the play end to end, much less among a company of their peers. Prospects for the future success of Active Analysis can be put at risk with a mismanaged introduction at this critical time, and there is still plenty of time for the actors to accomplish what is necessary. The director only needs to say as little as possible and maintain the right pace. In that way, even rehearsal of a long play will not bore the actors and the accumulated impressions will become safely deposited in the storehouse of their imaginations.

First reading of the play with the actors

Traditionally, the first reading of the play is done at the table, but for Active Analysis it can be more effective if the actors experience the first reading on their feet, moving around the rehearsal space in intuitive groupings. A physical experience of the first reading introduces the actors to a feeling of 'analyzing' the play psychophysically, instead of only mentally, which is inevitable if readings are undertaken exclusively at the table. Whatever the case may be, after the first reading the actors need to say a few words about their personal impressions free of premature directorial 'corrections'.

After this, the director talks briefly and concisely about his/her impressions of the play, its theme, and its artistic features. Then the subject shifts to similarly concise descriptions of the major characters. The actors also need to be cautioned at the outset about the army of clichés that are certain to appear when developing their characters, especially with one of Shakespeare's plays.

Besides the ever-present danger of clichés, sometimes actors can perform rather abstractly, not considering deeply enough how to behave in the specific given circumstances, that is, how *contemporary* people behave in analogous circumstances. This sort of discussion is a useful prologue to the kind of thinking – 'me' living truthfully in the given circumstances of another person – the actors will encounter throughout Active Analysis. Stanislavsky famously said that theatre has been called upon to reveal 'the life of the human spirit', and to do so it is necessary to reimagine that spirit internally in contemporary terms, not those of the past. When performers approach their roles by means of their own current sensibilities, it is possible to obtain the kind of results that Stanislavsky was striving for with Active Analysis. However, if roles are seen only as an opportunity for displaying historical or rhetorical erudition, then very little of the contemporary human spirit is likely to result. In the hands of a knowledgeable director, Active Analysis is capable of checking problems like these before they become habitual.

First episode (1.1.1–20): Introduction to the etude process

The first scene of *Midsummer* (1.1) consists of four brief episodes.[1] Since it is best to work with Active Analysis in short passages, each of these episodes offers a convenient way to begin the rehearsal phase Active Analysis.

At a brief table period, the actors familiarize themselves with the episode's external actions, framing event and character behaviours. At this point, the 'secret plan' that Stanislavsky referred to in his conversation with Zon warrants a word of explanation. Active Analysis requires directors to prepare for etudes with additional pre-rehearsal studies and a special kind of preparative attitude. The pre-episode studies consist of reexamining the passages for the upcoming rehearsal as specifically as possible, but – and here is the important point – avoiding the temptation to inform the actors of everything the director has discovered about the passage. Thus, the director's plan remains 'secret', in a manner of speaking. This strategy is not intended to manoeuver the actors into guessing what the director is thinking, but to empower the actors to take responsibility for their own work. Listening respectfully to their ideas, the director asks questions of the actors that require the utmost concrete answers. The director checks the specificity and accuracy of the actors' thoughts, changing his/her own previous night's homework if an actor suggests something more interesting and accurate. What is called for in this phase of Active Analysis is the free play of the *actor's* imaginations. Keeping the director's plan quietly in the background for the time being ensures that his/her ideas will not influence the actors too early, such that unintentionally their own creative imaginations might be inhibited.

The actors determine that the first episode is a meeting of three characters – Theseus, Hippolyta and Philostrate. That Theseus fell in love with Hippolyta on the battlefield and now he plans to celebrate their marriage. In fact, he is so impatient to do so that he instructs Philostrate to move the annual spring festivities one day ahead. The episode concludes with a few lines in which Theseus explains these plans to Hippolyta. The actors determine the framing event to be an announcement and they provisionally title the episode 'a royal announcement'.

From the table work, the actor playing Theseus knows the framing event and sequence of external actions for the scene. The actors playing Hippolyta and Philostrate have their own sequences and their own meanings. It is necessary for Theseus to praise, instruct and then romance. Hippolyta supports, concurs and acknowledges. Philostrate attends, acknowledges and then ensures.

Sitting at the table with their eyes fixed on the script cannot be very conducive to the emergence of living meaning and feelings. Shakespeare's text will be learned later, but at this point, it is possible for the actors to use their own words. So, the director says to the actors, 'Get up from the table and act the scene'. He/she is asking them to improvise an etude, or sketch, approximating the text with their own words and basing their behaviour on their knowledge of the framing event and the related external actions of their characters. Naturally, they will say, 'How can we act it? We don't know the words'. 'But you know the framing event don't you?' the director says. 'If not, we can go over it again. But you have already analyzed your character's external actions and the framing event, too, haven't you? Now you can go on stage and try to get oriented to the space, and then make your entrances.' They go on stage, try to get oriented to the space, and then make their entrances. On their feet, it is already more interesting for the actors because they can check whether their table analysis was sufficiently specific and perceptive. Moreover, when the etude begins, the director is already checking to see whether they are correctly carrying out the actions they talked about in the preceding table discussion.

Their first etude is done very simply. Philostrate enters and waits 'respectfully' for the arrival of Theseus and Hippolyta, who enter and stand 'majestically' while Theseus makes his announcement. Philostrate exits and Theseus says a few words 'affectionately' to Hippolyta. However, the etude has not provided an interesting solution to the episode. Something elusive is still missing. For the most part, early attempts at etudes are frustrating experiences, as the actors attempt for the first time to grapple with the complexities of the action and an emerging awareness of their personal responsibility in this process. After all, they are experiencing the action directly, person-to-person with their partners, and – this is the scary part – without the support of a script in hand. Moreover, it will be necessary for the actors to come to terms with a familiar mental obstacle: he/she worries, 'What should I do next?' They worry about forgetting something, which of course they always will do initially, because they have only brought with them from the table what they understood spontaneously and what stuck in their memories. The director offers words of reassurance that disappointment with etude outcomes is to be expected at this early point. After a few more tries, the feeling of being 'a stranger in a strange land' will disappear, replaced by a refreshing feeling of creative freedom. The actors only need to go back to the table and read the episode again to make better etudes and become comfortable with the feeling of being genuinely themselves on stage.

Having experienced a new awareness of their personal accountability for the future success of the production, the actors inevitably commence to pay closer attention to the text and think more precisely about the director's questions. At the table, it is noticed that two remarkable characters are about to get married, and it should be interesting to see how they behave at this important moment in their lives. The first etude has shown only how the scene needs to be understood 'in general', but this kind of tersely efficient summary seldom happens in real life. After all, the meaning of a scene is not only in the words but also in the action. There is the logic of the text, of course, but there is also the logic of the subtext. There should be no exceptions allowing the actors just to recite the lines to the audience by merely informing them of everything the author has written in the text.

The question for the director continually to ask is, 'What is really happening in this episode?' Duke Theseus of Athens is impatient to marry Hippolyta, Queen of the Amazons, an event that will take place in four days, on the first night of the new moon during the annual 'rite of spring'. He instructs the Master of Revels to 'Stir up the Athenian youth to merriments', to make sure the citizens of Athens are in a cheerful mood and ready for the wedding. But why is Theseus so eager to speed up the wedding, and in this particular manner? There is no pressing need for hurry here. After all, Hippolyta is obligated to marry him according to the aristocratic rules of war. Another puzzle is Hippolyta's relative silence in this episode. She speaks so little and so ambivalently that one might believe she is opposed to marrying Theseus and is assenting only from a sense of obligation. Moreover, why precisely is Philostrate present? Naturally, it is important for him to manage the plans for the wedding, but everyone in Athens is familiar with the annual spring celebrations. Especially the Athenian youth, for whom the rites of spring are a holiday of lovemaking. The upcoming marriage of Theseus and Hippolyta is not a secret either.

After all, there was a war with the Amazons recently, and Athens won. Moreover, a royal wedding will add even more enjoyment to both the victory celebration and the rites of spring.

There are times in life when one person converses openly and the other responds, as it were, distractedly. This other person's conversation contains some sort of secondary issue, while the primary issue lies somewhere in the area of the other person's personal ideas and concerns. That could be what is happening here. What was overlooked in the initial etude is the fact that Hippolyta is an Amazon, the leader of a nation of fierce female warriors. Amazons were an exclusively female society that mated with men solely for the purpose of procreation. (Male children were given away to foreigners.) Therefore, for Hippolyta the idea of marriage to a man is not only unfamiliar but also literally unimaginable. Metaphorically speaking, she is from another planet. It is no wonder she is reticent about marrying Theseus. She must *carefully assess her new situation* to learn how women and men 'in love' behave on this strange new 'planet'.

The key to the episode lies the fact that Theseus has previously detected her reticence, and now he seeks *to reassure her that love between women and men can be a happy experience.* The warrior in him defeated her in battle; now the lover in him needs *to win her love.* There is also the question of his desire *to change his life from that of a warrior to that of a lover and a civic leader as well.* Will he be able to persuade Hippolyta of the sincerity of his intentions? The political future of Athens depends on it.

To further these goals, his instructions to Philostrate must be done before Hippolyta. He feels the need *to do something new and unexpected with the goal of demonstrating his love in addition to his change of temperament.* He will cancel the solemn day of fasting that customarily precedes the festive rites of spring, and commence the festivities today, immediately. Philostrate is speechless, of course (imagine all the arrangements that have to be changed at the last minute), but the important thing for Theseus is that Hippolyta's reticence must be converted to sympathetic approval to forestall any possible second thoughts on her part.

This new awareness of the episode reminds us of something in the director's Action Analysis earlier, namely the special nature of an 'event' in the context of Active Analysis. The framing event turns out to be more specific than a 'royal announcement'; it is now, let us say, 'a surprising change of plans'. Imagine Amazon Hippolyta's bewilderment when this man says to her: 'I've got a surprise for you; we're getting married even earlier!' Additional etudes and visits back to the table reveal that Theseus wants *to charm and reassure Hippolyta, who is uneasy about what is to come;* and that Hippolyta wants *to assess the intentions of Theseus, who appears to her to be unusually enthusiastic about what is to come.*

This is how it is possible for a simple event to become more psychologically nuanced by means of Active Analysis. Moreover, all this is quite practical to accomplish through etudes and narrowly focused table work. If the actors forget the sequence of actions in an etude, it is only necessary to prompt them from the side. The text is sitting next to the director and, with one eye on the actors and the other on the text, the actors will not be allowed to make a mistake in this respect. The director can stop them any time they stray from the logic of the action. The only necessity is for the actors to understand the framing event and its related actions and then try to carry them out. Etudes ensure that the actors comprehend and express what lies beneath the text and not merely on the surface of it. After all, beneath the text is where behaviour exists, the actions of human beings. Once this goal is passably accomplished, etudes for the given episode are ended, and rehearsal can move forward to comparable work on the next episode.

Exercise

Choose one of the secondary plots to develop directorially. Proceed to work up the first episode of this plot by means of table work alternating with etudes in the manner explained above. Compare this experience with that of the episode from the main plot just now treated. What were the similarities? The differences? How did the actors respond to their first experience with etudes? How did your first directorial experience with etudes affect your own thinking? Was anything discovered about Shakespeare's manner of playwriting that may have been previously undetected?

Etude possibilities for scenes not in the play

Obviously, etudes are intended for scenes from the play itself. However, plays also contain scenes that are not formally stated in the text. This includes scenes referenced, implied, or inferred and whose content contributes to scenes that are formally stated. Such scenes contain events in the sense used in this book, that is, occurrences that take place for first time or last time, occurrences that normally would not or should not happen in the lives of the characters. Examples from the first episode include:

- Theseus falling in love with Hippolyta on the battlefield.

- Theseus escorting Hippolyta to Athens, where he shows her around the city, shows her his palace, and introduces her to the household staff and her personal quarters.

- The first time Theseus begins to sense reticence in Hippolyta's behaviour.

- Philostrate receiving the order from Theseus to be present for an important announcement. Alternatively, Theseus seeking Philostrate's advice about how to reassure Hippolyta of the sincerity of his feelings for her. (In this case, Philostrate would already know about the changes of plans, which would obviously influence both of their behaviours in this episode.)

There are multiple opportunities in *Midsummer* for etudes of such scenes. There is no official 'text' for such episodes aside from implications in or inferences from the text of the play. All the same, the guidelines for the etudes are identical to those for episodes stated in the text. As with events from the text itself, here too the framing event and its related actions must be specified prior to commencing each etude. By their very nature, however, etudes from scenes not in the play cannot always be as accurate or logical as those for scenes actually in the play, though they can be of significant practical value to the actors nonetheless. Etudes for scenes *not* in the play fill out behavioural gaps whose content will inevitably augment scenes actually *in* the play, even influencing scenes beyond those from which the devised scenes have emerged.

Second episode (1.1.21–129): The subtext and the feeling of empowerment

At first glance, there does not appear to be as much to consider at the table in this episode before attempting an etude. Angry voices are heard; Egeus, Hermia, Lysander and Demetrius enter. They have been arguing ever since they left Egeus's house a short while ago, perhaps arguing as well with palace attendants, who would not wish to interrupt the Duke at this time, despite the fact that Egeus is an important member of the Athenian ruling class. We know that Egeus came here for one final attempt to persuade his daughter to marry Demetrius. Why else would he trouble the Duke with a family problem at such an inappropriate time? We learn that Demetrius had been courting Helena, but recently he threw her over for Hermia and now he has Egeus's approval to marry Hermia. This, plus the fact that Theseus has already been somewhat concerned about Demetrius's conduct, is all we learn about him in this episode. We also learn that Lysander has been courting Hermia with love songs, tokens of affection, and gifts of flowers and candy. He has won her heart, which is more than can be said for Demetrius. Theseus's concerns about his upcoming wedding, carried forward from the previous episode, would probably cause him to consider Hermia a problem child. He might be thinking, 'Let's settle this trivial affair quickly, so that I can get on with my own plans, which are far more important at this moment.'

Equipped with this information, the actors are eager to finish the table analysis and move on to etudes. There seems to be no additional subtext or concealed meanings to prevent them from doing so. Immediately, however, the first etude runs into the same problem that occurred in the previous episode. Namely, the framing event of 'a royal petition' proves unsatisfactory and a straightforward expression of the text is uninteresting because something elusive remains unexpressed.

To seek the answer, Active Analysis necessitates another visit to the table to find what was overlooked in the first attempt. Further study of the episode reveals that Hermia's heartfelt appeal unexpectedly touches a nerve with Theseus about his own 'forced marriage' to Hippolyta. What is more, Hippolyta notices this. Egeus's paternal rights and Hermia's love for Lysander now become more than a trivial annoyance. There are larger issues at stake, such as Theseus's wish to mitigate Hippolyta's reticence, start a new life for both of them, and possibly even work in partnership with her toward developing a more liberal-minded Athens. The actors can see how Theseus must be careful about what he says in front of Hippolyta in this situation.

Consequently, to demonstrate to Hippolyta his sympathy for Hermia, Theseus impulsively adds the four-day interval of the spring festival as a waiting period for Hermia to make up her mind. No reaction from Hippolyta. Then he modifies the death penalty with an option for Hermia to become a votaress of the virgin goddess Diana (patron of the Amazons) and spend the rest of her life cloistered. Still no reaction. Hippolyta may be pleased about Theseus's sensitivity toward Hermia's feelings, but now she is upset from his reference to the 'barren' life of an unmarried woman, which Hippolyta takes as a veiled criticism of her way of life as an Amazon. Moreover, Egeus is upset by this turn of events as well. The Duke has not exactly said no to his petition, but he has not exactly said yes either. In other words, both Hippolyta and Egeus are both brooding over Theseus's actions. So sullen are they that Theseus insists that they pull themselves together: 'Come, my Hippolyta: what cheer, my love? [. . .] Demetrius and Egeus, go along.' To which Egeus tersely responds, 'With duty and desire we follow you,' while Hippolyta says – nothing. They exit, leaving the room ominously empty for Hermia and Lysander to consider the gravity of their situation.

The added information from this round of table work includes significant subtext as well as adding more meaning to text itself, so the actors are ready for another etude. Without further help from the director, the relationship between Theseus and Hippolyta immediately begins to reflect what was just learned at the table and therefore the etude becomes more complex and interesting. In addition, the etude visibly improves the feeling of empowerment in the actors themselves. Without prompting from the director, they are beginning to ask questions about embryonic feelings that arise in them during the etude. In other words, they have begun to 'analyze on their feet', which of course is the basic premise of Active Analysis as well as its creative aim. The actors' notional feelings may or may not prove to be relevant in the episode, but on their own, they choose to return to the table and find out for themselves.

Not surprisingly, the actors discover something more in the text that addresses a question overlooked before. Now that Theseus sees Egeus and Hermia together with her suitors, Demetrius and Lysander, he begins to understand the rumours of discord he had heard earlier (offstage) concerning one of Athens's leading families. ('I must confess that I have heard so much, / And with Demetrius thought to have spoke thereof;' [1.1.113–116]). Previously, Theseus had planned to talk to Demetrius about it because he knows Demetrius's history of boorishly treating women, and Theseus therefore sensed that Demetrius might be the source of the discord. This information sheds significant additional light on the situation. If Egeus has been misled by Demetrius, then his paternal rights may have no basis in law here after all. Therefore, Theseus must prevent Egeus from making a fatal mistake in the event that subsequent facts prove he was misinformed about Demetrius's actions. This new fact changes the essence of the framing event from 'a royal petition' to that of 'a distraught father'. Theseus has to deal with two problems at once. He must demonstrate to Hippolyta his sensitivity to love in general and to Hermia's feelings in particular *and* he must persuade Egeus to settle down and wait until all the facts are known (or until the young lovers resolve the situation among themselves).

To make all this happen, the actors need to go on stage once again and commit themselves to another etude. Commit *all* of themselves, which means their entire body, speech, feelings, imagination, everything to the very end, just as though it were happening with the actual participants in real life. They may not express everything as completely and specifically as the director could wish, but in any case, they must take action and *do* something that reveals their newly acquired knowledge of the episode. It is important to recognize that up to now these activities have taken place with minimal direct information from the director.

Exercise

Proceed to the next episode of the secondary plot selected for study. This time, pay particular attention to the actors' comfort level with the process, the ease or perhaps unease with which they move back and forth between table work and etudes. Naturally, some actors will be more at ease than others will with this approach. How is this ease or unease specifically revealed in their etude enactments and their comportment at the table? What thought-provoking or perhaps challenging traits in them as individuals are discovered by dint of this private directorial assessment? Now the director can begin to see some signs of the path in which the character played by each actor may or may not develop, and therefore plan accordingly.

Etude possibilities for scenes not in the play

- Demetrius jilting 'clingy' Helena.

- Demetrius 'falling in love' with Hermia, attempting to win her affections, and being rejected.

- Demetrius obtaining Egeus's approval to marry Hermia.

- Egeus informing Hermia that she must marry Demetrius.

- Hermia informing Lysander of her father's demand.

- Hermia and Lysander persuading Egeus to change his mind.

Third episode (1.1.130–182) : The theme and the director's 'secret plan'[2]

The actors have been making substantial progress with the play and with their grasp of the empowerment potentials of Active Analysis. The next episode offers the possibility of further development in both respects.

At the table, we know that the Duke has threatened Hermia with death or a lifetime of confinement if she fails to obey the law; now she and Lysander are intentionally left alone by Theseus to come to terms with their situation. The actors conclude that Lysander is consoling Hermia. He says that true love like theirs is always challenging and surrounded by unexpected dangers – 'The course of true love never did run smooth.' (1.1.136) – and he lists some of them. Hermia duly recognizes his examples as their own dangers as well. Then Lysander suggests they should run away from Athens and get married. Hermia says she is ready for anything – *as long as he remains faithful to her.* The scene is no more than two pages long, yet it contains an entire history of two young people overcoming fear and the eternal law of love. They do not actually overcome this law, but learn something new and profound about it in a moment of despair.

The actors determine that the framing event is 'frightened criminals', and the action consists of the two characters assessing the gravity of their situation, and then deciding to run away together. Thus, Hermia laments, and then approves; Lysander consoles, and then inspires. Using this sequence of actions, the actors go on stage to perform an etude. Predictably, the etude does not provide an interesting solution. What occurs is simply a 'conversation scene', where two actors stand side by side exchanging sad comments, and then they are no longer sad and decide to escape.

By common agreement among the actors, it is necessary to return to the table for more detailed study of the text. The psychological complexity of the episode comes as a surprise. Lysander explains their predicament as a universal law of love, so he feels that Hermia is mistaken to react in a way that 'the roses [on her cheeks] do fade so fast . . .' 'Here you and I are defying the way of the world,' he seems to say, 'and you are feeling sorry for yourself!' He must console her, but how many ways of consoling can there be? It can be done angrily, tenderly, coarsely, silently, impatiently and more.

Also noticed at the table are Hermia's responses. They appear to be fairly disengaged, continually interrupting Lysander's consolations. He repeatedly seeks to console her, but for some reason she does not seem to be listening. She agrees with his thoughts about love's difficulties, but she is oddly abstracted from the specific situation in which they are trapped. Studying the text more closely, the actors discover the subtext. It appears that Hermia is turning pale from compassion, not self-pity. While Lysander talks about material obstacles to love (class, age, social pressure, war, sickness, death), Hermia is saddened about the adversities that confront true lovers everywhere. She identifies herself with everyone who shares their misfortune. One actor at the table recalls that Shakespeare provides a similarly wide-ranging worldview in the lives of certain other characters too, notably in two well-known soliloquies. Juliet ('O Romeo, Romeo, Wherefore art thou Romeo?'); Hamlet ('To be or not to be, that is the question.') At some of the most dramatic of turning points, Shakespeare's characters express a worldview without selfishness or ego. The passage studied at the table shows that Hermia expresses a similar worldview: ('If then true lovers have been ever cross'd, / It stands as an edict in destiny.' [1.1.152–153]). This misfortune is not only theirs but also is shared by persecuted lovers everywhere on earth.

Promptly feeling braver about themselves and their plight, Hermia and Lysander determine that to suffer does not mean to obey. They will not merely escape; they will challenge the eternal law of love and bear it on their shoulders as a sign of defiance. At this point, the episode takes a turn, and Lysander provides a way for them to show the courage of their convictions: 'That is right, Hermia,' he seems to say. 'We have clashed with the eternal law of love, and I know what we can do about it: we can run away. We have overcome the eternal law of love and now we will be able to live happily ever after', or so they would like to believe.

Another etude follows. The actors visualize and physicalize this new awareness, and therefore their etude changes substantially for the better. Their behaviour has adjusted and the previous lack of interesting dramatic action has been transformed into a lively and complex episode. It turns out that while searching for a way out of their own misfortunes, Lysander and Hermia are capable of talking about surprisingly elevated and complex issues.

This is a critical moment in rehearsal, because the current episode also happens to be a significant turning point in the play's action; it has something special to say about the whole play. So the actors are asked to return to the table once more. This time the director's questions are less about the individual episode than about the world of the play in total. The director asks, 'What is the meaning of this episode in the overall context of the play?' In this kind of episode – an episode with significant implications vis-à-vis the entire play – it is appropriate for the director to reveal selected information from the 'secret plan'. Of course, this plan is 'secret' simply because the director has not spoken openly about it with the actors, but has only put forward necessary parts of it to guide the early phases of etudes and table work.

The director explains that in this episode Shakespeare creates a certain 'object lesson' wherein Lysander's *sentimental opinion of love* ('Love conquers all things.')[3] is set against the *unsentimental law of love* ('The course of true love never did run smooth'). This opposition combines to form the play's theme, which in turn sets all in motion all the secondary plots as well. The actors readily understand how Hermia and Lysander would like their love to be problem-free, but the director suggests that this theme informs the relationship between Theseus and Hippolyta as well as Oberon and Titania. Furthermore, Puck debunks the gullibility of mortals 'in love' ('Shall we their fond pageant see? / Lord, what fools these mortal be!' [3.2.114–115]), and the Mechanicals' effort to produce a tragedy about love results in a comedy. Each scene of the main and secondary plots is an object lesson reflecting a different facet of Lysander's proverb. Indeed, the entire play is composed of a variety of such facets, as we have said.

This new awareness has significant value practical for the actors. Now they are ready, even eager, to come to terms with the theme, an issue they would usually relinquish to the director. From a pedagogical perspective, they can begin to understand how the theme of the play operates as a subtextual current flowing beneath the words and influencing their expression. From a performance perspective, the theme sticks in the actors' imaginations because it has been explained in concrete terms that have a reckonable application in their work. Moreover, the theme was explained not in lengthy directorial table discourse during the first week, but precisely at that point in rehearsal when the actors were best equipped to deal with it on their own terms.

Exercise

Naturally, secondary plots contain fewer events than the main plot. They do, however, contain a beginning, middle, and end as described in the eponymous section earlier. The middle episode of most plots is usually a significant turning point, and for that reason the thematic nucleus of the specified plot is likely to be more conspicuous in that episode.

Select the middle episode of one of the secondary plots to rehearse at the table and with etudes. Take note of the characters' actions, and the actors' capacity for living through the episode's framing event accurately and interestingly. Then turn to the theme of the specified plot itself, how it is expressed in the text and subtext of the episode, and in what way it echoes the main theme of the play, whether directly, indirectly, parodically, or ironically. After another round of table work and etudes, check to see how the actors' work has been influenced by this thematic awareness.

Etude possibilities for scenes not in the play

- Lysander's previous visits to the home of his aunt. What facts have occasioned their visits? What has their relationship been like up to this point?

- Hermia and Lysander each gathering their things in preparation to leave home, their meeting after that, and the beginning of their escape through the forest.

- Hermia and Lysander imagining their arrival at the home of his aunt, their wedding and future developments in their marriage.

- Egeus, Demetrius and Theseus and Hippolyta each receiving the news of Hermia and Lysander's escape.

Fourth episode (1.1.183–231): Operative role of the theme, the personality of the actors, and clusters of psychology

Identifying the theme is important, of course, but finding its specific connections with the other episodes in the play is equally important. The upcoming episode with Helena, Hermia, and Lysander offers the now customary opportunity for table work and etudes. It also offers an opportunity for the actors to understand how the theme produces both playable dramatic values *and* connections with other episodes.

The actors conclude that this episode consists of two parts. In the first part, Hermia's closest friend, Helena, bursts in full of pain and insults, accusing Hermia of stealing Demetrius away from her. She scolds Hermia, and then reluctantly assents to her friend's explanation. Hermia calms Helena down, and then reassures her. Lysander supports Hermia throughout. In the second part of the episode, Helena reassesses her relationship with Demetrius and decides to take action on her own.

The actors are beginning to understand that etudes require a sense of faith in the actions to be undertaken as well as a sense of truth in expressing them. This much is evident in the first attempt. Nevertheless, for whatever reason, something still gets in the actors' way. Some things are clear, but other things remain obscure. Even for Hermia to greet Helena turns out to be a complicated psychological issue. This episode ought to be more than simply bickering rivals followed by confusing words about love.

In Active Analysis, much depends on how the director perceives the personality of the actors. One actor naturally expresses a certain quality, another actor a different quality, and these differences can change something in the execution of the etude and ultimately in the production. On the other hand, it is pointless to push an actor toward something that is not characteristic of his/her nature, even if it is technically correct in terms of the play itself. This does not mean Active Analysis makes it necessary to adapt the interpretation of a play to the actors. Not at all. Correctly understood and carried out by means of etudes and carefully focused table work, Active Analysis intrinsically provides a way of approaching a play that expresses its meaning *in harmony with the self-evident individuality of each actor.*

Back at the table, the director asks again, what is really happening in this episode. Recalling the previous episode about a love problem that besets Hermia and Lysander, the actors quickly recognize that the present episode is about a love problem that besets Helena and the absent Demetrius. Stereotypically, Helena is sad and angry throughout this episode from the feeling of being unloved. Upon closer reading, the actors become aware of quite a few zigzags, clusters of psychology, that were previously undetected. First, Hermia has unintentionally wounded Helena's pride with the word 'fair' (fortunate, happy). Then Helena tells her it is cruel to greet her in such a thoughtless manner. Then Hermia insists she is not making fun of Helena, and that she is not to blame for Demetrius falling in love with her. Hermia has tried to put him off, but he continues to pursue her even though his advances have been stoutly refused. Helena remains skeptical. Then, to set her straight, Hermia and Lysander are obliged to disclose their escape plan to her, which obviously means that Demetrius will never see Hermia again. Helena finally grasps the true nature of the situation. And then her friends depart, leaving her alone on stage. Seven distinct clusters of psychology.

The zigzags discovered here reveal this episode's connections with other scenes in the play. In the process of Helena reassessing her situation, she is also going into more detail about the fact that 'The course of true love never did run smooth'. First, she stops to reassess her situation seriously, that is, to reconsider her love relationship with Demetrius. She thinks about Hermia's happiness for being loved and about her own unhappiness for being unloved. Her pain is caused by this sense of rejection. Then she realizes how irrational and capricious love is, and how a lover's imagination can transform one thing into another. Love has persuaded Demetrius to desert Helena and idolize Hermia despite her rejection, she says, and likewise love has persuaded Helena to idolize Demetrius despite his rejection. In other words, until a short while ago, Demetrius idolized Helena; today he idolizes Hermia and rejects Helena. Then she begins to understand why Cupid is always depicted as blind: it is precisely because lovers have no sense of judgement; and always depicted as an infant precisely because lovers can be so easily fooled.

Now, having sorted out the real-world complexities of love, Helena decides that manipulation is the only way to get what she wants, namely, to force Demetrius to recognize the emotional blind alley into which love has led him. She will inform him that Hermia has fled with Lysander into the forest. Naturally, Demetrius will rush into the forest to find Hermia. Helena will follow him there and lead him astray. And when he fails to find Hermia, he will inevitably return to Helena's waiting arms. Anyhow, she would like to believe this would be so.

Helena chooses the path of 'gender-role defiance', as we might say today. She will be the hunter and Demetrius the hunted in order *to save Demetrius from himself.* Twenty-six lines of text containing six dense clusters of psychology. Owing to this 'betrayal friendship' Helena has revealed how 'The course of true love never did run smooth' connects with the mass of other mistakes made by the characters who are or would wish to be in love.

Some of the psychological dots may remain unconnected, but at this point, the actors understand and believe in the psychological correctness of all these zigzags well enough to undertake further etudes. Happily, a palpable awareness of the theme is beginning to show up in their intonations, gestures, facial expressions, and groupings. On their own, unprompted by the director, they are beginning to grasp how Active Analysis works in the best interests of the actors.

Exercise

The quarrel between Oberon and Titania over their adoptive son has triggered a disruption in the course of nature. Clearly, their love has not been 'running smoothly' for a long time. This much is obvious even in a cursory reading of their episodes. What is not so readily apparent is that they are the only married couple in the play. Hermia, Lysander, Demetrius and Helena are in the courtship phase of love. Theseus and Hippolyta are about to get married comparatively late in life. Pyramus and Thisbe are lovers from literature, and the Mechanicals are indifferent to a tragic love story taking place in their midst. Why is it thematically significant for Oberon and Titania to be married and be involved as well in a child-custody battle? Close attention to this question can reveal the thematic variant in this episode and therefore its latent connection with the rest of the play. Clearly, the answer must lie somewhere in the subtext. What exactly does the subtext consist of in this episode and how does it show itself through the text? Notice, for example, Titania's long speeches set against Oberon's equally long silences. How does awareness of the subtext increase the playable dramatic values in the associated etudes?

Etude possibilities for scenes not in the play

- Hermia and Helena's previous get-togethers as close friends. How did their friendship begin? What are the qualities that bind them together in this friendship?

- Helena learns about Egeus's plans for Hermia to marry Demetrius, thus realizing that Hermia has 'betrayed' her. Where does she obtain this information and from whom?

- Hermia imagines how her 'intervention plan' for Demetrius will play out.

Fifth episode (1.2): Operative role of the through action, controlled guessing, and gestation time

A similar survey of table work and etudes for the rest of the play is not possible in the space allotted here. All the same, it will be worthwhile to look at the next scene for an example of how Active Analysis functions with an episode that seems to be fairly isolated from the through-action of the play. This process will take extra time because the episode is more dramaturgically refined than it appears to be, which is also what accounts for its apparent isolation.

The Mechanicals are rehearsing a play they hope to perform before the Duke.[4] At the table, the dramatic content of the episode looks simple enough. The framing event is 'an amateur casting session'. Quince distributes the roles, Bottom takes over the spotlight, and they all plan to meet in the forest the next night to rehearse. Not surprisingly, parody wins out in the ensuing etude because the characters' innocent lack of ability is so tempting to laugh at. However, even now the director understands there is potentially as much meaning as nonsense in this episode. So the actors are asked to return to the table and look for any kind of refinement they can find in Shakespeare's 'rough theatre' (Peter Brook's term).[5] After closer attention to the episode, it appears that the humour may not always be so primitively farcical after all; it comes from the Mechanicals' ignorance of the actor's work. After all, they face the same problems that we as directors and actors would probably face if we needed to make someone a gift and tried to construct it with materials from the local hardware store. This new awareness ought to clarify and deepen the actors' understanding of the episode's framing event; otherwise, the outcome will be the same as before.

The actors continue their table searches, except that now they search for the behaviour beneath the words as well. There are close guesses, guesses farther away and fresh original guesses. It is like target practice, and no one has hit the target yet. Great concentration, plus experience, is necessary. They guess just about anything imaginable, guess around it and near it. But what really happens in the episode, the actors find hard to grasp at the table. Nonetheless, this type of controlled guessing needs to persist, since it is a significant pedagogical feature of Active Analysis. Controlled guessing is intended to foster the practice of seeing precisely what is essential in an episode and what is not.

With judicious prompting from the director's 'secret plan'. the actors can discover what happens in the episode relatively by themselves. The Mechanicals want to make the best possible impression on the Duke, but neither Quince nor Bottom trusts the other to carry this off satisfactorily. Quince considers himself the expert here. He thought up the project, adapted the script, and assembled the cast. In his mind, Bottom is a recent arrival. His talent for the melodramatic will be of use in the lead role, of course, but he also threatens to ruin the project's chances for success before the Duke.

In contrast, Bottom considers himself the only real expert in this situation. The text suggests that he has seen a few plays and may even have some friends who are actors. For those reasons, he knows how to direct a play! Thus, Bottom feels that he can 'talk the talk and walk the walk'. Whereas, he feels that Quince is clueless about such 'professional insider' matters and will make a mess of the whole project. The through-action of the episode is this: Quince is battling against Bottom over control of their project. The framing event turns out to be more specific than an amateur casting session; it is, one might say, 'An urgent game of thrones'. The combatants are proletarians, not royals of course, but they still play the game with utmost urgency and earnestness. On the other hand, the stakes of this game are by no means dangerous or life threatening and this fact exposes comic potentials of which the combatants themselves are unaware.

Since connection of this episode with the play's through-action is ironic, not just typical, it is therefore less immediately obvious than in earlier episodes. The Mechanicals are preparing a play that is itself an illustration of the theme of *Midsummer*. 'The course of true love never did run smooth,' albeit from a tragic perspective since death is very real in this story. The Mechanicals are indifferent to its tragic content, however, and so their behaviour is pointedly in contrast to what would be expected in such a situation. The great comic actor W. C. Fields once said, 'Comedy is tragedy happening to someone else'. His observation certainly holds true for this episode. The misfortunes of Pyramus and Thisbe are of little concern to the Mechanicals, but merely '. . . a very good piece of work . . . and a merry'. They are totally unmoved by the tragedy of love they hope to perform. Lysander is battling against the enemies of romantic love; meanwhile, the Mechanicals are indifferent to, if not openly laughing at, such concerns. In both plots, the principals are responding much more intensely than is justified by the circumstances. They are reacting to their situations so strongly and so often that one starts to suspect the rationality of their perceptions.

At this point in the table analysis, everything in the episode appears to be understood by the actors, and yet when they try to express all this in an etude, still nothing interesting results. They know what to feel, hear, and touch, but the melody they hear in their heads still must be played. It is like they studied the music very well, but now it is time to pick up the instrument and play it. They will need lots of time to learn how to hold the instrument, and so on. Even if they have 'absolute pitch', it will take more 'gestation time' for the performance to sound anything like what they heard in their imagination. Not least for a scene containing the kind of refined humour identified here.

Exercise

This analysis of the first Mechanicals' scene could lead one to question the other scenes with the Mechanicals, notably the finale (5.1). Assume that the theme, 'The course of true love never did run smooth', applies to the *entire* play; that it is consistent not only with Acts 1–4 but also Act 5. Accordingly, the play performed by the Mechanicals at the end may not be entirely clowning. Nor may the reactions of the on-stage spectators be entirely trivial asides either. This exercise is intended to test that assumption by means of Active Analysis.

Director Anatoly Efros writes about a Polish director who produced this scene in such a way that the on-stage spectators teared-up as they watched it. A recent New York production by director-choreographer Julie Taymor also expressed an ironic understanding of the scene.[6] This point of view might help to explain the interchanges among the couples watching the play, which typically come off awkwardly. Being newly married, they might reasonably feel that all the obstacles to their love have been overcome, and therefore from now on everything will 'run smooth' for them. Yet statistics tell us that more than half of all marriages *today* end in divorce. Perhaps the Mechanicals' performance of *Pyramus and Thisbe* could be taken as a sign that further 'lessons about love' are waiting in the shadows for these newlyweds. Why are Hermia and Helena silent throughout this scene, and what is the motive behind Hippolyta's sympathy for Thisbe's plight? Could the honeymoons be over even before they begin?

Furthermore, does the tragic ending of *Pyramus and Thisbe* suggest that the opposing views of love in *Midsummer* do not resolve each other in comforting harmony as is usually the case in performance? Is there any evidence that the characters have learned from their mistakes or that they will not repeat them over and over again without thinking? Notice that the harmony between the two opposing views of love in the previous scenes (4.1&2) was not brought about by any sort of new self-awareness on the part of the characters but only by the magic of theatre.

Is such an interpretation accurate? Plausible? If so, could the Mechanicals exemplify certain present-day potentials in *Midsummer* much in the same way as Brecht has done with the characters in his plays? Could they expose a special meaning behind the conflict, as fables are intended to do? Of course, it is easy to *say* something, anything, about a play, but in the end, it still needs to be tested through table analysis and expressed through etudes. And it is easy to get lost in these places too, not only because of the generations of literary judgements attached to

Shakespeare's play(s) but also here because the meaning and action in the finale of *Midsummer* are more elusive than those in earlier scenes. Put these questions to the test by means of table work alternating with etudes.

Etude possibilities for scenes not in the play

- Quince learning about the contest to select a play for the Duke's wedding celebrations and deciding to adapt *Pyramus and Thisbe* for this purpose.

- Quince soliciting the assistance of his comrades for the project.

- Each of the Mechanicals departing from home, work, or leisure to meet at Quince's home to learn more about the project.

- Where the participants go after leaving Quince's house.

6

Further Active Analysis and Testing

Now the moment has arrived when the entire play has been intellectually examined and acted out more or less satisfactorily in etudes. This moment will end the second period of work – the period of initial analysis and testing. Now another period begins. This will be the period of analysis and testing of challenging episodes.

Psychological obstacles

As we have seen, Shakespeare can be surprisingly difficult from a psychological point of view. For example, the 'love transformations' that *Midsummer* depends on for much of its appeal. Here is a list of them:

- Demetrius unexpectedly falls in love with Hermia and out of love with Helena (before the play begins).

- Lysander unexpectedly falls in love with Helena and out of love with Hermia.

- Bottom's head is unexpectedly changed into that of a donkey (off stage).

- Titania unexpectedly falls in love with an animal and out of love with her adopted son.

- Demetrius unexpectedly falls back in love with Helena and out of love with Hermia.

- Bottom is unexpectedly changed back into his original form.

- Titania unexpectedly falls back in love with Oberon.

The transformations in *Midsummer* are extreme. Nevertheless, as clusters of psychology, extreme or otherwise, transformations need to be analyzed, tested and expressed through performance, which necessitates the search for internal plausibility. How to find this plausibility in extreme transformations such as those in *Midsummer*?

We will look at the transformation episode between Bottom and Titania as a model for working with the others.[1] Even at this late date in rehearsals, instructions will not be given to the actors through directorial speeches, but psycho-physically through the reciprocal process of table work and etudes. At the table, the actors quickly decide on the content: Titania wakes up and falls in 'love at first sight' with a strange forest creature. The actors perform the initial etude hurriedly, and it comes out uninterestingly, as might be expected. Titania awakes, runs to Bottom, embraces him, and says some poetic words about love. However, there is more than this going on in the director's 'secret plan' for the episode. Back at the table, the director encourages the actors to 'micro-analyze' this passage. It happens that Shakespeare actually offers plenty of feelings and ideas here for the actors. Something awakens Titania. Oberon has bewitched her to fall in love with the first 'somebody' she sees upon awakening. The first thing she sees (actually hears) is a singing forest creature. The first thing she says is, 'What angel wakes me from my flowery bed?' (3.1.124). Meantime, this creature is singing something, which to her is strange itself on the face of it. There is something strange about a forest creature who sings. Particularly if the creature is a transformed Mechanical by the name of Bottom, who does not understand that he has become a half-human donkey and is singing so his friends will not think he is afraid.

Precisely at this moment, Titania wakes up and engages in a conversation with the creature. What is the psychological structure of this tiny episode? First, a woman hears a voice, but she does not see the creature involved. Second, she sees him and asks him to repeat his song. Third, 'Oh, he's leaving!' 'Don't leave, stay here with me!' is the fourth. Four separate clusters of psychology, four zigzags in the action.

But there are two characters in the scene. The bewitched woman and the creature she falls in love with. He is also bewitched, and suddenly some strange forest woman is hanging on him. That is to say, something extremely improbable is happening to both of them. How would we ourselves behave if we suddenly encountered something similarly improbable? Let us say we are sitting in the park near a cat, it is behind you; you saw it and unconsciously you sensed how it looks and behaves. When you turn around, a human being is standing there instead of a cat! You might say to yourself, 'This can't be happening! Either something is not right with me, or something strange is happening around here'. The process of *assessing the improbability* begins.

This process is different for each character in this episode. At the sight of Titania, the donkey-human does not evaluate himself but the person who is reacting to him, and he remembers that a few moments ago his companions wanted to make an ass out of him. Titania, on the other hand, is involved in the process of falling in love, albeit involuntarily. Because of the magic nectar, she is falling in love with a romantic dream, an idealized (fetishized) image. Thus, 'meeting with a surprising stranger' forms the revised framing event of the episode. They are both assessing the situation: something strange is happening!

It is important not to rush the zigzags in this episode or any similarly extreme episode. If the actors can take their time with such micro-processes, then the larger process of *assessing the specific nature of the transformation* can reveal itself. Additionally, this episode needs to be treated not only in itself but also as a facet of the performance's broader meaning. Looking for this connection back at the table, the actors notice that Titania speaks about the moon and flowers at the end of the episode ('The moon, methinks, looks with a watery eye, / And when she weeps, weeps every little flower, / Lamenting some enforced chastity.' [3.1.191–193]). They also remember earlier examples of enforced chastity in the play – Hippolyta's Amazon heritage and the threat of the convent hanging over Hermia's head. Titania's lament references the forbidden love latent throughout this episode, which connects with the theme of the play.

On average, performances tend to attribute such extreme transformations to Shakespearean verbal mannerism, clichéd stage business, or stage tradition. Bearing this in mind, it may be necessary to explore similarly tradition-laden episodes more than the usual number of times. When the actors are unable to get hold of anything strong and dramatic after two or three attempts, then the number of attempts can double or triple. Nonetheless, the overall approach to especially challenging episodes remains the same: a combination of table work and etudes when and as often as necessary. Clichéd notions can only be exposed by scrupulous rechecking of individual psychological clusters. Indeed, each of the love transformations in *Midsummer* merits the kind of patient microanalysis undertaken here.

Exercise

Earlier in 3.2 Puck has mischievously transformed Bottom's head into that of an ass, and the Mechanicals are stunned by Bottom's changed appearance. Study the on-stage components of this transformation episode by means of table work and etudes. For each character in the episode, identify the clusters of psychology and determine the path of action. In short, search for internal plausibility in the episode. In what specific ways, if any, are the outcomes different from what was expected at the beginning?

Etude possibilities for scenes not in the play

- Puck transforms Bottom's head into that of a donkey.
- Oberon places magic nectar on Titania's eyelids.

Mental analysis and etudes ought to reveal that neither of these off-stage episodes is as simple as it appears at first glance.

Blocking

Nemirovich-Danchenko once said that blocking should envelop the action like a glove. Accurate and expressive blocking starts from the psychological structure created by the playwright. As the external form of that psychology, blocking logically ought to develop through the actors themselves. If the director has accurately felt and thought out the episodes beforehand, a rough form of blocking necessarily evolves of itself in the etudes. Even so, the blocking that evolves in rehearsal seldom appears without change in the final production. The director typically adds or subtracts something to make the blocking more precise and expressive.

This is where another aspect of Active Analysis comes into play. On one hand, every director should possess the requisite blocking skills for the profession: awareness of what an event is and how it controls the action; the ability to understand the production as a whole; to develop the appropriate scenery, costumes, lighting, sound and makeup with the designers; to determine the relationship among acting, staging and meaning, etc. On the other hand, the director using Active Analysis also needs to be a good teacher, counsellor, an expert in perceiving tiny signs in the actors' speech and action. Furthermore, since Active Analysis obliges the director to restrain from interrupting the actors with 'corrections' for as long and as much as possible, the director must therefore be a calculatingly patient person all the way through the rehearsal period.

Physical characterization

Active Analysis cannot address all the issues of the actor without exception, of course. However, there is one more challenge that Active Analysis can provide the resources to address.

Actors and directors sometimes develop an immediate attraction for certain external features of a character. The essence of a character has not been analyzed, yet its external features are immediately considered. A character has to limp, wear glasses, or speak with a strong voice, because this is what is done by certain people similar to the character and whom, perhaps, the director or actor knows personally or by reputation. Nevertheless, impulsive decisions of this type are usually too simple; they can blemish a performance that would otherwise be consistently justified internally.

Several years ago one of the theatres produced *The Elephant Man* by Bernard Pomerance.[2] In the eponymous role of John Merrick, a very good actor slurred his speech, awkwardly positioned his back and arms, and walked with an unusual limp. Yet the inner life of the character was hard to recognize, perhaps even absent. Another production, Moliere's *A Doctor in Spite of Himself*, was directed by an expert on the subject of *commedia dell'arte*. As might be expected, the production was a scrupulous illustration of that historical style. The actors diligently employed all the well-known postures and stage business pictured in theatre history books. Aside from the picture-book identities of the characters, however, who they were or why the director chose to depict them that way remained unclear. In other words, physical characteristics can be devised for a character through brainwork alone and be obvious to everyone, but often the results can wind up distracting from the inner life of the characters.

By contrast, Marlon Brando's performance of Don Vito Corleone in Francis Ford Coppola's film, *The Godfather* is a successful example of physical characterization.[3] Everybody praised Brando's characterization. It was not distracting; on the contrary, it produced an awareness of his character's inner life. Audiences followed his character's ideas and feelings, while observing only parenthetically his restrained and courteous demeanour, stooped posture, shuffling walk, meticulous clothing and grooming, the distinctive way of rubbing his extravagant jowls with the backs of his fingers, and above all, his raspy voice, a crowning feature that expanded the whole remarkable portrait. The result was a physical characterization of historical influence. Naturally, Active Analysis cannot ensure that actors will be capable of developing characterizations as remarkable as Brando's was, but the holistic, psycho-physical view point of Active Analysis can ensure that preconceived ideas about physical characterization are at least minimalized, if not completely eliminated.

Everyone has his/her own unique way of speaking, gesturing and walking, of course. All the same, on stage the inner life of a character ought to be more interesting and thought provoking. In fact, Stanislavsky recommended that physical characterization ought to be a finishing touch, not a starting point.[4] Otherwise, it can become an unnecessary distraction for the actor.

7

Conclusion: Rehearsal Realities

We have been studying Active Analysis with the intention of utilizing it from beginning to end, throughout the entire rehearsal period of a play. While this goal is obviously ideal, it nevertheless takes loads of time, and time is a commodity in short supply at most theatres and drama schools where directors might be reading this book. In the theatres of Russia and Eastern Europe, where Active Analysis was born and has been in use for a long time, rehearsals can often extend as long as it takes a production to achieve its goals. To be sure, most of these theatres operate by means of a 'rotating repertory' arrangement, which is intrinsically time consuming since several plays are always in rehearsal at the same time that several others are in production. Moreover, rotating repertory is an expensive and resource-intensive play production system. Be that as it may, 'flex time' is built in to this system by default, rendering it reasonably conformable to the needs of Active Analysis when it is called for. Meantime, most Western theatres and drama schools operate according to a set series of uninterrupted performances, or 'straight runs', which is a more concentrated and economical rehearsal system. Nonetheless, the characteristically efficient use of time in this arrangement has its disadvantages. The constant time pressure resulting from the necessity of a prescheduled opening night, for example, can have an unwelcome influence on what should ideally be a measured and patient process of creative gestation.

This is the challenge faced by a director wishing to make the most of Active Analysis in a straight-run system. There is simply not enough time to work with this method as Stanislavsky intended, that is, without the obligatory time limitations of a straight-run production calendar. There are exceptions, of course. Groups of like-minded theatre practitioners have always found and will continue to find the time and resources necessary to carry out their creative goals outside the constraints of the traditional system of play production. But what is to be done by a director who would like to work with Active Analysis while also continuing to work within straight-run rehearsal and production conditions?

The main thing for this director is to be mindful of the basic structure of Active Analysis. The ultimate goal is to ensure that the events in a play are explicitly present in the actors' imaginations and accounted for dramatically in their behaviour on stage. The basic structure of Active Analysis, therefore, depends on knowledge of events in the technical sense used here, identification of their logical sequence, and then detection of the framing event governing the participants' behaviour therein. The search for events is accomplished by studying brief passages of the text at the table, followed by an approximation of the text improvised by the actors in etudes. If at first the actors are unable to live accurately and truthfully in the events, then they repeat both activities, each alternating with the other, until, guided with sensitivity by the director's 'secret plan', the actors can satisfactorily come to terms with the events on stage, before our eyes.

As for the practice of etudes as such, the actors must be allowed to improvise the action in their own words, but they must nevertheless *do* something so the director can confirm the accuracy and plausibility of their understanding. Despite appearances, however, etudes are not an end in themselves, and strictly speaking, they only need to be employed as necessary for a given episode. Anyhow, after the events are sufficiently understood and expressed, the actors can begin to assimilate the author's text gradually during the course of rehearsals. The words of the text will come easily enough if the events have been understood consistent with the logic of the play's action. Sometimes the actors' approximate words continue longer than necessary, which can create problems in maintaining the accuracy of the author's text. Whatever happens, the director or a production assistant is always there to ensure the eventual accuracy of the text.

A director choosing to work with Active Analysis must be infinitely patient and stubbornly insistent that the actors both know *and* express the framing event established for every episode. To accomplish this with Active Analysis requires the actors to either possess or be disposed to cultivate a capacity for continuous improvisation. Unfortunately, this is where Active Analysis can sometimes encounter opposition from veteran actors. Their background and habits can lead to disapproval of this approach, accepting it on the outside perhaps, but resisting it on the inside. These actors will obtain little if any benefit from Active Analysis. They should probably be left to work in their own customary ways, without worrying about Active Analysis. Over time, they may come to appreciate the advantages of Active Analysis and even make an effort to work within its parameters. It is not always about experience, however. Beginning and apprentice actors can be ill disposed to Active Analysis because it requires skill and adaptability, thinking on one's feet among and before one's peers.

A director's plan is mandatory, of course, and the director must always be much more than merely a step ahead of the actors in this respect. The director determines the framing events, theme, through-action, etc. and holds them in reserve in a 'secret plan', but he/she also must cooperate in good conscience with the actors on the details of understanding, amending and implementing this provisional plan. It is not feasible and even creatively harmful for the director to strategize too much in advance how the search will develop with the specific actors involved.

True, the gist of Active Analysis is likely to be present in any sort of correct rehearsal work. Then again, if a director is already achieving good results instinctively, perhaps Active Analysis could help to produce even better results. Initially, Active Analysis can be tried on a few episodes from a play currently in rehearsal, while the rest of the play is rehearsed in the customary manner. In this way, a director can test the process and see how it works for him/herself personally.

§

This completes an account of one director's experience using the Method of Active Analysis with a classic play. It is hoped that this account will persuade the persuadable that Active Analysis really has something to offer, and that, with a little bit of effort, thoughtful directors and teachers can profit from its methods.

The following account by Maria Knebel is considered the formative work on Active Analysis, providing virtually all the essential information about its history, pedagogy, practice, and creative potentials.

PART TWO

Active Analysis of the Play and the Role[1]

Preface

Interest in the creative legacy of Stanislavsky has increased considerably over the years. Many theoretical books about his ideas have appeared, numerous articles devoted to various parts of his system, and, finally, most important, publication of his works.

All this is extremely gratifying, since the serious periodic study of a master's precepts enriches the creative consciousness of theatre practitioners and advances artistic thinking in all places. Today there is virtually no part of the country [now we could say the world] where theatre workers do not read Stanislavsky, try to understand his creative principles, and study the theoretical foundations of the profession.

All the same, we cannot forget that these are only the first steps in this important matter. Lately, a number of questions have been identified that merit additional theoretical development. But even though we argue much and often about the theoretical positions of Stanislavsky's system, nonetheless, the practical methodology of theatre, that is, the direct creative processes themselves are not the subject of such discussions often enough. We directors apply Stanislavsky's final discoveries in our own ways, everyone according to their understanding of and relation to these questions. As a result, confusion and contradictions arise. The actor, passing from theatre to theatre and working with different directors (and students studying with different teachers), often receives contradictory instructions that interfere with skills that are often still embryonic. Too frequently, crude simplifications circulate under the guise of Stanislavsky's innovative rehearsal process, which in turn generates discouragement and undermines the credibility of Stanislavsky's once-experimental technique.

We seem to be willing to write articles on certain controversial questions of his system, yet we are hesitant to raise the curtain from our personal creative laboratories. We tend to share our own experience and our own store of creative knowledge very sparingly. We talk a lot about how we understand Stanislavsky intellectually, but little and equivocally about how we actually work in relation to Stanislavsky.

We can find the most convincing arguments supporting one or another's opinion and call for the assistance of all our well-known aesthetic concepts, but until we can support our theoretical conclusions with practical examples explaining how we actually work, the murkiness surrounding Stanislavsky's final searches will not go away. Consequently, his concepts will continue to be shrouded in mystery for the vast majority of theatre practitioners. Accordingly, I would like to tell you how I understand and use Stanislavsky's new method in the creation of my performances and in the process of teaching my students at GITIS.

Maria Knebel

1

General Principles of
Active Analysis

I want to explain the rehearsal method proposed by Stanislavsky –
the so-called Method of Active Analysis. Briefly, the essence of this
method is that in the early stages of preparation the play is not
rehearsed at the table as usual, but after a certain amount of preliminary
analysis it is analyzed in terms of action through etudes using improvised
text. These etudes, or sketches, serve as stepping-stones that lead the
actor towards creative assimilation of the author's text, that is, to the
author's words as the principal means of stage expressiveness.

In the latter period of his life, Stanislavsky acknowledged the need
to reconsider the earlier method of rehearsals developed by himself
and Nemirovich-Danchenko and afterwards supported by the
established practice of the Moscow Art Theatre.

As we know, the Moscow Art Theatre initiated the practice of
starting off rehearsals with meticulous analysis at the table, where
the play's entire ideological and artistic structure was exposed to
careful scrutiny, encompassing all the internal motives, implications,
relationships, characters, through-action and super-objective of the
production. This 'table period' of rehearsals played an important role
in the development of our art. It taught the actor to penetrate deeply
into dramatic structure, to reveal the play's 'subtext', and to reach the
subtlest stirrings of the human spirit. It contributed to the formation
of a new type of actor, for whom creation of 'the life of human spirit'
became the essence and purpose of creative work.

Long ago, this reformist practice of the Moscow Art Theatre had
already become the common property of virtually every theatre in

Russia. Today, at even the smallest theatres, the rehearsal process begins with analysis of the play according to its internal lines, which the actor masters beforehand at the table. But while creativity in the theatre increased and respect for the rehearsal method established by the Moscow Art Theatre grew stronger and turned into an unshakable custom, Stanislavsky, with an insight unique to him, had already begun to recognize a number of its darker aspects.

One of the new forms of work proposed by Stanislavsky for elimination of these darker aspects was analysis of the play in terms of its action. This method is connected with a number of questions regarding the basic principles of theatre and can only be understood in light of the entire body of Stanislavsky's teachings.

Throughout his entire life, Stanislavsky dreamed of the thinking actor, the actor-creator who knows how to interpret his own work and live actively in the given circumstances of a role. Any reduction of the actor's independence in the theatre seemed like a disturbing symptom to Stanislavsky. And the moment he began to notice this, he began to engage in a fierce struggle against it.

During the latest period of his work as a director, he began to notice with embarrassment that the actor had become like clay in his hands.

There was a time when this would have pleased Stanislavsky, but later in life, he saw the tendency of the actor to follow a director's orders unthinkingly as an obstacle to the further progress of the art. As soon as passivity arises in the actor, he easily gets used to the idea that everything will be solved for him by the director. 'Steered' by the director from play to play, the actor gradually comes to the position of 'Lead me!' with regard to the director. Only in the final stages before opening night does the actor suddenly remember that he needs to act something, and then he begins quickly, with painful tension, sometimes in mechanical fashion, to squeeze himself into a role. Here too occurs that same dislocation, that same violation of the creative process against which Stanislavsky so passionately struggled.

Proclaiming the actor's passivity an evil in art, Stanislavsky, with ruthless self-criticism, restrained a tendency in himself to cover the sins of the actor's inertness with virtuosities from the director's professional imaginings. He declared war against passivity in the theatre, in whatever forms it appeared.

Role of the director

By imposing more requirements on the actor, however, Stanislavsky never intended to reduce the responsibilities of the director. He searched for a harmonious union of the wills of the actor and the director in the process of creating a performance, and for accurate, creatively favourable relations between them.

At the first rehearsal of a new play, the director is normally much more prepared than the actor is. The director, as expected, works ahead of the company. His imagination has already grasped an image of the future performance, its scenery design, and its 'seed'.[1] He knows why he is directing the play and he determines the entire performance as a whole, not just for one role, but for the entire assembly of characters in the play. Accordingly, when meeting the actors, even the most patient director hurries and rushes ahead, thereby violating the natural encounter of the actor with the role, imposing his own vision on the performers and restraining the actor's creative independence.

However, Stanislavsky wanted to teach directors to place the actor in conditions that would develop the actor's feeling of personal responsibility for the role from the very beginning. He passionately defended the purity and spontaneity of the actor's first impression of the play,[2] attaching significance even to how and who first acquaints the actors with the play, that is, whether the director presents questions, adaptations and adjustments at the first reading that could hinder the independent perceptions of the actor.

For the same reasons, Stanislavsky warned directors against presentation of a detailed explication of the play at the very beginning of work.

Details from the life, period, style, literary and critical researches – all this will be necessary for the actor in due time, that is, when he plunges into the dramaturgic elements of the material. At the first meetings – when the actor still knows almost nothing about the character and the director overloads the actor's imagination with all sorts of general information – the actor usually accepts the director's comments coolly, rationally. He finds himself facing a large amount of diverse and wide-ranging information. But since there is not yet enough information relevant to him creatively, he looks hungrily for some special path that will lead him to that mysterious stranger whose words are printed in the script. After all, in a few months, the actor must be able to speak these words as himself!

Stanislavsky taught us as directors to make careful use of this trait in the actor and to be able to use it for the development of the actor's own initiative and commitment.

Some observers have said that in the last years of Stanislavsky's life he allegedly urged directors to prepare for the future production only together with actors. This assertion is devoid of any foundation, in my view, and is very far from what Stanislavsky sought from his student-directors in practice.

The notion that Stanislavsky did not prepare for rehearsals has spawned a group of 'geniuses', who think they do not need to prepare for a future performance. After all, they will be able to create it together with the actors. One of Stanislavsky's remarks when he was working on *The Inspector General* at his studio generated this notion. In reply to the question from an actor: 'What will we do next?' he answered, 'I don't know. I don't know anything'. Naive people took Stanislavsky's pedagogical strategy as an authentic response. They forgot that prior to the studio performance he had directed *The Inspector General* twice, the last time with Michael Chekhov playing Khlestakov. They forgot that Stanislavsky knew the play perfectly well.

Implementation of Active Analysis depends first of all on the director. The organization of rehearsals is in his hands. He has a responsibility to construct the rehearsal process in the spirit of Stanislavsky's new method. And this demands large and complex preliminary work.

The director who underestimates this responsibility, who is not prepared for the requirements of this new practical methodology at the beginning of rehearsals, will soon discover that the creative team, like a ship without a helmsman, will continually lose its direction, veer off course, and waste valuable rehearsal time.

On the other hand, the director who is fond of method for the sake of method – forgetting the purpose for which it exists, that is, realization of the meaning of the performance – will inevitably arrive at empty formalism.[3]

Naturally, the director's initial ideas about the play and performance will be enriched during the course of work, changing as needed depending on what the actors bring with themselves and what their individual qualities are. But it is one thing to develop a plan and quite another not to have one. A director's plan, interpretation, the identity of the director, the features of his style – none of these concepts was ever invalidated by Stanislavsky.

Introducing this new method of work, he emphasized that the director should possess the kind of pedagogical tact that will allow him to reveal his knowledge of the play not 'in general', but only when it is genuinely necessary for the actor.

Accordingly, Stanislavsky raised the question of method, about a certain kind of pedagogical ingenuity wherein the director's view of the role and the play is not 'imposed' upon the actors, but subtly revises and leads them towards a unification of their independent searches. The director is an interpreter, a mirror, the organizer of the performance – all three functions of the director identified by Nemirovich-Danchenko continue to operate in the new rehearsal system.[4]

Unity of mental and physical life

The struggle against actorly passivity was not the only reason for a change in the previous rehearsal method. No less important was the fact that the previous method of rehearsal unthinkingly sanctions an artificial life-contradicting gap between the mental and physical sides of the actor in the given circumstances of the play.

In table work the actor only comes to understand the psychology of the character intellectually, accumulating only the character's 'internal baggage'; and then, transferring to the material conditions of the stage, he switches his attention to the 'life of a human body', the physical side of his existence. Only in the material conditions of the stage does he begin to look for the physical life of his character and bring it into harmony with the world of the character's thoughts and feelings. Yet how much time has passed, how much effort has been expended, trying to connect these two elements, without which there is no truly authentic human being!

A number of articles have been published about the influence of Ivan Pavlov's theory of conditioning on the formation of Stanislavsky's system.[5] Actually, it seems to me, the issue is more complicated than that. Stanislavsky did not know Pavlov's theory (although he did read Ivan Setchenov[6]). Nevertheless, I think it often happens that great ideas, ideas about the modern perception of reality, quite often emerge simultaneously. And this is what happened with Stanislavsky. He concluded that somewhere, somehow we had separated the mental existence of a role from that of the physical. At the beginning of his Moscow Art Theatre's endeavours, for example, Stanislavsky devised the staging and scenery for *The Seagull* without even being present at Nemirovich-Danchenko's rehearsals. He devised the staging by going through the physical mode to get to the psychological.

Later on, Stanislavsky began to focus his attention on the need for disclosing the mentality of the characters, their inner experiences, and consequently human psychology became the cornerstone. Only after refining all the psychological pathways did Stanislavsky recommence his searches for external forms, searches for the physical behaviour of the characters, and searches for the stage settings. Gradually he concluded that both sides of a role must be connected, not only in the process of embodiment but also in the process of analysis itself.

Was Stanislavsky indifferent to the physical behaviour of the actor before this? Of course not. It must be remembered that the efforts of Stanislavsky and Nemirovich-Danchenko ensured that the actor mastered a character through the unity of its psychological and physical traits. The activities of daily life, the authenticity of everything surrounding the human being, the atmosphere of the action – all this permeated their work from the outset and created the special charm of Moscow Art Theatre performances.

Stanislavsky's later doctrines about the physical life of a character relied on his own independent and extensive searches in that direction.

Meanwhile, he did not overlook the gap he perceived between the period when the actor analyzes the mental side of a role and when he switches to the development of its physical side. In the old rehearsal method – when many hours were devoted to theoretical analysis of the play and the role, discussions about action, and thoughts about 'what *he* [the character] is like' – the actor became accustomed to seeing the character separate from himself, outside of himself, involuntarily thinking of the character as 'him' instead of 'me'.[7] Consequently, the actual transition to the role, the merger with the role, presented great difficulties for the actor.

Eliminating this gap, Stanislavsky concisely formulated a law about the psychophysical unity of the actor's creative process. He also raised the question of how to realize this unity in day-to-day practice so that it embraced all the actors' creative activities – from initial analysis up to and including performance.

The position of the author's text

Stanislavsky attached primary significance to the text on stage. He considered verbal action to be the primary type of action in performance and the primary means for expressing the author's thoughts. He demanded that on stage, as in life, the text must not exist in isolation, but within the complex psychophysical existence of the human being, inseparable from the entire intellectual, emotional and physical range of human expression.

But the text cannot be mastered organically until the entire complex structure of the subtext is worked out, and until the actor masters all the psychological clues that lead him to the author's text. Stanislavsky concluded that when the actor tries to use the author's text immediately, that is, when he starts simply to learn the text by itself, he is thereby deprived of the possibility of achieving a profounder awareness of the subtext.

Meanwhile, in the earlier method of rehearsal, the actors go directly to the author's text from the outset, and furthermore they only read the play according to their own roles today, tomorrow and every day. Consequently, the text – which has not yet been supported with internal impulses and not yet connected with the entire fullness of human life on stage – already starts to enter into the memory of the actor mechanically and imprints itself 'on the muscles of the tongue', as Stanislavsky liked to say. As a result, quite often in performance the text does not emerge as a living reaction to the thoughts of the partner. What emerges is neither action nor even a willed act, but only the reply to a remark, a 'cue', which the actor unconsciously clings to as a simple mechanical signal.

Furthermore, the mechanically memorized text often serves as a kind of protective screen for the actor, behind which it is possible not to think, not to feel, not to work, and not to exist. Compelled to create under the watchful control of many eyes and lacking in creative capability thanks to scores of external circumstances, the actor instinctively looks for ways not to show what is really on his mind, and he is often protected for this very purpose by the author's text. To tell the truth, many things give the actor away in such cases: a blank look, an unjustified gesture and languid or inexact intonations. Furthermore, how much precious time is consumed trying to ensure that the actor speaks one or another line with the proper 'fullness' in order to say something he is not even ready for!

It seems a paradox at first, but the text often 'demagnetizes' the actors [i.e. removes their 'attractive' personalities]. Even the most active performers do not comprehend the given circumstances of the play deeply enough because they know that the vocabulary of the author is ready at their disposal, a vocabulary where everything is already expressed and everything is already formulated. Meantime, it is enough just to say the words, and then, in due time, they will be filled with the appropriate internal contents.

Stanislavsky greatly appreciated the freshness of the text and its function as a 'lure' for the actor. He believed that an actor's indifference to the author's text, often coming even earlier than the birth of the actual performance, is always a bad omen for the fate of that performance and its hoped-for longevity on the stage. He concluded that it is not possible to rehearse a play according to its text until the huge world of external and internal motives that gives birth to the text has been mastered.

Etudes

For that reason, Stanislavsky rebelled against the earlier way of preparing a performance, which he helped to originate himself, and he began instead to defend passionately a new way in which the play is analyzed in action, in etudes [sketches] with an improvised text.

At this point, it is necessary to pause for a disclaimer. Because of Stanislavsky's final searches into the actor's milieu, a myth was born regarding the so-called 'elimination of table work'. In fact, while changing the manner of analyzing the play, Stanislavsky never suggested eliminating or simplifying analysis itself. On the contrary, the etude method also serves the purpose of deepening play analysis and increasing its efficiency. Moreover, the practice of 'table work' continues in the new method, only it works in a different way – the play is not read simply according to its roles, but repeatedly addressed holistically, both at the table and with etudes.

Those directors who consider it possible to begin rehearsing a play without analysis debase Stanislavsky in the crudest way and violate his creative precepts. This discussion, therefore, is not about the elimination of the table period, but about *a change in the way a play is analyzed* [italics added].

Active Analysis is a new practice, experimental.[8] And just as with any new practice, a vulgarized and simplified approach is extremely dangerous. Although Active Analysis is accessible to every average actor's understanding, actively facilitates the creation of characterization and the performance as a whole, and accelerates the creative process, nevertheless, this does not mean that mastering it is an easy matter. There is nothing more unjustified than the idea that if a role is analyzed by means of etudes, it is then ready for performance before an audience. Stanislavsky's new method is, in the exact sense of the word, a method of analysis, as opposed to the embodiment of a character. In the process of analysis, however, there are also elements of embodiment. But only elements. At times, they can be unusually interesting and unexpected. Occasionally it happens that something found in the very first etude illuminates a role with a feature so essential that it complements the entire period of work.

Stanislavsky saw the purpose of Active Analysis not to conclude with a characterization emerging in finished form, but to put into operation not only the brain but also the entire organism, the entire being of the actor immediately from the outset, and to help him feel 'himself in the role and the role in himself' more quickly. Only when the actor sufficiently masters the given circumstances in etudes can he begin to create freely. This is already a lot, but it is still very far from actually creating a finished role.

Stanislavsky compared the improvised text born in the actor during an etude to those innumerable draft copies done by a writer when refining his work. The actor would follow the same path. 'In the improvisations you should reach the "seed" of the author's main thought,[9] the thought that led him to write this piece of the text,' Stanislavsky said to a group of young actors.[10]

Similarly, for a painter the etude [rough drawing] is an internal path to the painting, with the help of which the artist masters real life. With changes, many things found in an etude could eventually enter into a painting, but taken by itself, an etude is not yet a finished work of art.

The value of this new method is that it removes the wall between analysis and embodiment, which was artificially erected in the earlier rehearsal method. In the course of Active Analysis, the actor accumulates all the necessary elements for the embodiment of a character, and this transition is accomplished painlessly, smoothly, and without violating the actor's creative nature. Active Analysis is an organic process and therefore the shortest way to physical embodiment, which, from my point of view, is one of the strengths of this method.

The etude as a tool of creative practice is not new. Etudes were in use at the Moscow Art Theatre before Stanislavsky arrived at the idea of Active Analysis. They were used for investigating the background story of a role and for the events occurring between the acts. Working on a production of *The Inspector General*, Nemirovich-Danchenko rehearsed a scene called 'at the market', which we know is not present in Gogol's comedy.[11] The governor of the town went to the market, looked over stalls, looked at the goods, accepted payoffs from the merchants and generally put things in order. This scene helped the actor to find many essential character traits for the governor of a provincial town, which in turn appeared in a number of actions he performed in the play.

Nemirovich-Danchenko often employed etudes even during the middle period of rehearsal, when the actor had already developed his characterization. He suggested etudes on events that are not directly in the play in order to check how deeply the actor felt at home with the character he created, and how flexibly and freely he thought and performed from within his line of action.[12]

Without rejecting the usefulness of etudes like these, and continuing to use them whenever necessary, Stanislavsky suggested using etudes in the course of analysis of the events in the play, and from which etudes directly derive their outline.

The strength of this pedagogical device is that during etudes the play is studied more deeply than it is possible to do with table analysis alone. While learning the special world of the play, the actor almost immediately puts himself into the living conditions of the character and looks for practical ways to achieve rapport with it.

To create an etude about an event from the play and to find the sequence of actions for each character, it is necessary to undertake serious preparatory work.

After all, Active Analysis puts the actor in conditions where, for the time being, he substitutes his own text for the author's words, while simultaneously remaining faithful to the development of the author's thinking. The latter point is essential for the etude to be of real use for the actor. Inexact, vague ideas of the role or the play will inevitably lead the actor down a false path, force him to dodge and weave, to deviate, because he will be substituting his own casual ideas for the author's creative path and strategies.

To create an etude is no simple task. An etude demands a lot from the actor. The goal is achieved only when the actor makes direct contact with the play instead of withdrawing himself from it. And in order for this to happen, the actor should understand the main strategies and ideas put into the playwright's work.

Mental analysis

An important phase of work goes before the moment when the actor steps on stage to create an etude, a phase that Stanislavsky called 'mental analysis'.[13] 'Creative feeling is guided along the pathways prepared by mental analysis.'[14] The actor should observe this sequence during Active Analysis.

How did Stanislavsky imagine the period of 'mental analysis'? Among the numerous shared aims that illustrated the strong alliance between the views of Stanislavsky and Nemirovich-Danchenko was their concern that the actor should consider the entire role from the very first steps in a performance. Consequently, in the course of mastering a role, the actor proceeds from the general to the particular, from the essence to the details. With his usual integrity, Stanislavsky would not accept a performance deficient in organic unity, not subordinated to the main idea, and not penetrated by this idea from top to bottom, even if there were talented details in it. 'Break Apollo's statue into small pieces and show each one of them separately. The shards will hardly hold a viewer's attention', as he explained his antipathy to an actor's work deprived of organic unity.[15]

Developing these thoughts further, Stanislavsky created the principle of the 'two perspectives': the perspective of the actor and the perspective of the role – one of the most advanced and important concepts of his system.[16] It is aimed at the actor's habit of moving around in a role blindly, from fact to fact, from unit to unit, from action to action, without a clear aim and without an accurate vision of what the role should necessarily lead to. Indeed, the character cannot know what happens to him upon entering the flow of the play, nonetheless the actor is obliged to remember the result to which the author and director want to bring that character. The actor should proceed from this result and subordinate it to all the actions of his character. The perspective of the actor means the proper correlation of parts and the harmonious development of a characterization – with each step leading the character towards the super-objective.

Super-objective

By suggesting that the way to create a role is by subordinating it entirely to the super-objective, Stanislavsky also understood that it is only possible to define an authentic super-objective when the actor has already learned the contents of the play. He approached the act of finding the super-objective as a big, complex process. He could not accept definitions of the super-objective that were merely workable, merely general, and thus incapable of inspiring or exciting the actor. We still encounter such examples quite often in the course of work, using words that come from looking at a performance from the outside. A performance about courage, about friendship, about love, about the struggle between two factions – such definitions, though they may be true, are not capable of creating a role; they are too general [abstract] for the actor.

Certainly, after the first reading of the play, the actor acquires some vague feeling, a presentiment, of the thematic system of the performance and the perspective of the role. But this presentiment must be identified and developed – initially during the period of 'mental analysis' and then during etudes. Only at that point will the actor be able to find a concrete, practical guide for his behaviour on the way to the super-objective.

How should we approach a definition of the super-objective of the role and the play? Stanislavsky repeatedly stated that a true super-objective arises in the actor only when he manages to understand where the actions of his character lead. In other words, the actor moves towards the super-objective of the role by way of its through-action.[17] Action – this is what the actor needs to understand in his early approaches to understanding the play.

Action

The concept of action figures prominently in Stanislavsky's final searches. However, this does not mean the question of action was new for him and arose only in his later years.[18] It is only necessary to look closely at the number of such statements in his book, *My Life in Art,* and to re-read his directing journals to see how much attention Stanislavsky devoted to the question of action throughout various periods of his life.

The innovative value of Stanislavsky's late discoveries is that, while still considering action as the basis of the actor's creative process, he also thought about the series of activators that could lead to mastery of a scene by way of its action.

Earlier, while working under the direction of that same Stanislavsky, the actors were used to answering such questions as: 'What do you *want* in this episode?' In recent years, Stanislavsky began to focus attention on the question differently: 'What would you *do* if such and such happened?' The first question can easily pull the actor towards passivity, contemplation and force him to become isolated from the events that are taking place. The second question does incomparably more to activate the internal orientation of the actor, puts him in the territory of concrete action, and thereby helps him to learn the actions of his character.

Between 'I want' and 'I do' there is an essential difference. 'I want to go' or 'I go'. In 'I want', there is a passive element, but 'I do' means activity, usefulness and transition to a concrete environment. To accomplish this, however, it is necessary to know why you do it and for what purpose. Therefore 'I want' always exists because it arises the moment when 'I do' transfers the character to another plane, another world. Thus, some actors say 'I do', and others 'I want to do', meaning that one is acting and the other is only dreaming about acting, passive.

I think the future development of the theatre will depend to a great extent on the actors' mastery of the difficult unity between 'I want' and 'I do', that is, what 'I do' to achieve what 'I want'.

To the question 'What would you do if such and such happened?' the actor can answer only when he understands what takes place in the play, namely, the event that leads him to perform a given action or group of actions.[19]

Here Stanislavsky suggested that actors should begin their work on a play by studying the important events in the story that forms the basis of the plot. This allows the actor from the outset to grasp the essence of the role to a substantial degree through the development of the conflict. He learns to understand the play through its action and counteraction, and this brings him closer to the concrete super-objective of the role.

Stanislavsky cautioned that it is necessary to approach the definition of the super-objective very carefully. I often have to deal with directors' explications where super-objectives such as these are attempted: 'to build a nation', 'to create happiness for our citizens', etc.[20] Such abstract super-objectives could be suitable for many, many plays. We need a more concrete definition. When starting to work, the director should think about what this play says and what he, the director, hopes to say with it. At this juncture, universal concepts should be expressed with more concrete words and should rely on material that is in harmony with the actor's work.

When defining the super-objective, it is dangerous to take an excessively detached vision that does not really nourish the actor. Both in the definition of an event and in the definition of a super-objective, concreteness that nourishes the actor and director every minute and every second is necessary.

We should not forget Stanislavsky's basic propositions. First of all, that the super-objective should inspire the director and the actors in their creative work. Too often, a perfectly formulated super-objective is not felt in the performance. The director talks about the main idea and about the super-objective, but they are not sufficiently planted in the hearts of the actors. Consequently, by not being carried through all the actions and all the events, they lose their meaning. The director said that he wants to serve this play's main idea, but it remains only nearby but not yet *in* the performance.

Events

It is important to remember that each event generates a new action, which in turn generates a new event.[21]

Stanislavsky did not choose the event as the starting point for the work of the actor casually. He emphasized events for their complexity, since events are the shortest route to involve the actor in the world of the play. He said 'Look back at any stage of your life, remember what event was the main thing at this stage, and then at once you will understand how it was reflected in your relations with others.'[22] This, of course, is obvious to everyone. It is only necessary to remember what changes entered into one's life from the death of a loved one, a marriage, moving to another city, changing professions, the illness of the child, or the day a war began or the day of a great victory.

It is the same in drama. The tragedy of *Hamlet* begins with a basic event outside of Shakespeare's play – the death of the king. The death of the father foully killed by his brother and followed immediately by a change in the mother, who has become the wife of the murderer 'ere those shoes were old' – all this opened Hamlet's eyes to the world. These events led him to the conclusion, '. . . the time is out of joint', which produced both a furious desire to revenge the offenders and simultaneously a bitter awareness of the senselessness of revenge, paralyzing the will of the hero. They caused the entire sequence of bloody incidents that forms the outline of Shakespeare's tragedy.

Analysis of events is an important concept of the system. It is absolute because it starts with specific knowledge of the laws of drama, laws on which the greatest writers have constructed their works. Without events, without a chain of events, dramas do not happen, no matter what the genre is to which they may belong.

I consider the question of disclosing an event to be fundamental for contemporary theatre. Because how we further treat this question determines the direction in which theatre will develop.

Some say that we overload the actor with concepts such as 'the second plan'[23] and subtext and force him to analyze long chains of events. I believe such a viewpoint is self-indulgent. It impoverishes the theatre. A person cannot live without a past, and it is impossible for a character on stage not to have a past. We have a tendency, unfortunately, to say, 'All this is just bookishness! We do not need to argue about where a character comes from or whether he has a past. Let's just go ahead and "stage" the conflict or struggle in this episode'. And they start to 'stage' the conflict, but the audience sees that the characters are nothing but empty spirits for the simple reason that they entered merely from backstage and they will exit merely to return backstage.

The shipwreck that has thrown Viola into the fantastic country of Illyria, for example, makes the action of *Twelfth Night* possible. Even in those plays where external action, the external plot, seems to be absent, where everything is subordinated to the internal development, where, apparently, life is embodied in its ordinary daily flow – even then, events, the living communication of events, nourish themselves with the feelings, thoughts and experiences of the characters. The drama that has destroyed the illusory happiness of the Islayevs became possible in their quiet house and elegiac existence when a thirty-year-old woman placed a young teacher from another world between the two men who are equally devoted to her and equally distant from her. At that point, Turgenev's *A Month in the Country* was born. In *Uncle Vanya,* the same working purpose is carried out by Serebryakov's resignation and the subsequent arrival of the Serebryakovs to Uncle Vanya's estate, allowing Vanya to see in person the true, bourgeois essence of the professor, a sacrifice to which Vanya devoted his life. In *Three Sisters,* the arrival of the brigade to the provincial city has stirred up all the hopes and expectations of the Prozorovs, namely, their unrealizable dream of Moscow.

Great playwrights have known this law about the birth of action and have never violated it. Alternatively, we in the theatre quite often do so by starting to study the play neither from the large events nor from the chain of smaller events nourishing them, but merely by analyzing scene after scene, episode after episode, while missing the initial thread, the opening push.

The actor should closely study the entire chain of events that form the narrative structure of the drama, from outset to outcome.

These events – or as Stanislavsky called them, effective facts – form, so to speak, the skeleton, the framework upon which the writer constructed the play. It is necessary to be able to expose this framework, but this is only the first step in studying the play. The logic of the plot is an important thing in dramatic art, but taken by itself – separate from psychology, human relationships, characters, and the world of feelings – it inevitably becomes merely a formal process.

Some analysts say that by proposing events as the source of action and emphasizing the primacy of action, Stanislavsky ceased to take objectives [tasks] into consideration, that is, the purpose for which the character performs his actions. Stanislavsky said scores of times that action does not exist outside of motives, its nourishment, outside of those motives that push the character towards a given action. The essence of the character is revealed in his motives, and the range of his motives involves the entire range of the actor's behaviour.

Together with the question, 'What am I doing here?' another question should arise in the actor: 'Why am I doing so?' Only then will he manage to enter into the complex soul of the character and grasp the collective 'life of the human spirit' of his role.

Evaluation of facts and events

'Authentic drama, although it is expressed in the form of a given event', author Mikhail Saltykov-Schedrin writes, 'the latter only serves as an opportunity to finish those contradictions that nourished it long before the event itself, contradictions that are concealed in life and which gradually prepared the event from far away. Considered from the point of view of an event, the drama is the final word or, in some measure, a decisive turning point in some human life.'[24]

Beginning with study of the play according to its events, Stanislavsky, like Saltykov-Schedrin, considered them as 'turning points' in the life of a character. The actor should realize what part the given event, or a given fact, plays in this character's life, what behaviour it pushes the character towards, and what thoughts and feelings it arouses in him.

To evaluate one or another event in a play, Stanislavsky suggested mentally removing it, for example, by trying to imagine what would happen if a given character did not appear. What would happen, say, if Romeo did not appear at Capulet's ball just when it was arranged for Juliet to marry Paris – how would Juliet's fate be resolved? Obviously, she would have another destiny, rather sad, perhaps rather unfair, but not so tragic. There would be none of those flashes of insight or that new sense of independence that provoked Juliet's courageous actions.

Therefore, studying the play's events, the logic and sequence of the behaviours and actions of the character, the actor gradually starts to evaluate them and starts to realize the motives behind the actions of the character.

In the process of 'mental analysis', the skeleton of the play already starts to acquire living tissue for the actor. Usually after such analysis, the actor can already start to imagine what his character does in the play, what he aspires to, whom he struggles with, whom he associates with, and how he treats the other characters.

Stanislavsky wrote:

What does it mean to evaluate the facts and events in a play? It means to find the hidden sense in them, the spiritual essence, the degree of their value and influence. It means to dig under the external facts and events, to find there, under them, other, more important, deeply hidden, heartfelt events, perhaps generated by the most external fact.[25] It means to track the line of development for an external event and to feel the degree and nature of its influence, the direction and the line of striving for each of the characters; to learn the patterns of the many internal lines of the characters, their external collisions, crossings, textures, and their convergences and divergences, with the general aspirations of each towards his own living purpose. In a word, to evaluate the facts means to feel the internal structure of real human life. To evaluate the facts means to perform someone else's facts as one's own, the events of an entire life created by the poet. To evaluate the facts means finding a key to the secrets of the character's spiritual life hidden under the facts and the text.[26]

To see how actively the actors embodied the operational structure of the play, Stanislavsky suggested that each actor should recount the line of his role for the entire play, beginning to end. This is a very useful exercise because the attention of the actor necessarily concentrates not on what the character says, but precisely on how he acts, what he achieves, why he performs this or that action, that is, on the action and the motives. To recount the line of the role can be quite difficult for an actor. He is able to do it only when the logic and sequence of the events is already developed in his consciousness. And since this recounting is done by each of the actors while all the others are present, they can correct, argue and prompt each other. Thus, in the course of 'mental analysis', the entire company obtains a clear knowledge of the factual material in the play.

When the play is analyzed in this way, each actor separately and the company as a whole also approaches a definition of the super-objective of the play.[27] They have been guided by the material in the play, and they know the path of every character together with the chain of events belonging to him and his actions. Consequently, they can establish with remarkable accuracy what aspirations underlie these actions and what the main goal is for this person and this group of persons, and as a result, they can comprehend the meaning underlying the work as a whole.

Intellectual work on the play, its examination during the period of 'mental analysis', does not take very much rehearsal time. From the first meeting, the participants of the future performance have 'Ariadne's thread' in their hands,[28] namely, access to the play through its events, actions and behaviours, which puts them to work on firm ground at once. Naturally, everything depends on the complexity of the play and the richness of its internal development. In any case, the actors should not wander around through the play, wasting their time and energy on conversations about the play and its roles 'in general' (this has happened and continues to happen in the earlier method of work).

From the very first steps the actors plunge themselves into study of the concrete actions of the characters, studying the role not from piece to piece [unit to unit], not from scene to scene, but according to the major milestones of human life present in the structure of the play. From the very beginning of work, they learn the perspective [beginning, middle, and end] of the role and quickly become involved in advanced work by passing on to analysis of its details and examining them from the position of the main thing guiding their roles.

I will remind you once again: in the course 'mental analysis', the actors analyze the play, understand it, but do not rehearse it and do not read it with their own roles in mind.[29]

2

Details are Important

When the actor generally understands the effective line of a role, when he comes to understand the logic, sequence and value of the main facts of the characters' lives, we come back to the beginning of the play once again. Now, we start to study the text in more detail, not only the major milestones but also the smaller, minor events and associated objectives, and the actions.[1] In other words, everything that is necessary for the actor in an etude.

Further active analysis and testing

The goal at this point is to get as close to the play as possible, omitting nothing from its external and internal motives. Here we also identify such topics of conversation in the given passages as may be relevant to the actors' own lives. Otherwise, it will be problematic for the actor to improvise the text in such a way that their own words express the thoughts of the author.

But for the actor to be able simply to name this or that topic [of conversation in the text] is not enough for an etude. It is necessary to understand what role each topic plays in human life, why this topic arose in these circumstances, what gave birth to it at this moment, and what purpose the character has in mind when he comes up with this or that topic. And since the actor already knows the basic events of the play, knows the living purpose of the character, it then becomes less difficult for him to define which topics in a given conversation are decisive or central, and which are secondary, minor, or transient.

For example, the main engine of action in Moliere's play, *The Bourgeois Gentleman,* is the passionate desire of the bourgeois social climber, Jordain, to become a bona fide member of the aristocracy. All of Jordain's actions follow from this desire: his education in the 'wisdom' of the aristocracy, his clothing made by an 'upper-class' tailor, his attempt to obtain an upper-class mistress, and finally his scheme to marry his daughter to the son of a 'Turkish sultan'. All these actions reveal the essence of Jordain throughout the play.

When we began to sort out how we should proceed with Jordain at the Central Children's Theatre, we were convinced that the main thing exciting Jordain in terms of an event is Dorimene's impending and long-awaited arrival.

Jordain wants to be a nobleman to the tips of his fingers. His greatest dream is to have an upper-class mistress. If Dorimene appears to like him, it means he has thereby become a nobleman in the opinion of the world, or at least Jordain thinks so. The prospect of Dorimene's arrival is the basic event of his life today. Whatever Jordain does, he never for one minute loses sight of the fact that this will happen today, that today 'she' will come. This thought dictates a certain rhythm of behaviour for Jordain and a special greediness in the way he receives all the 'wisdom' with which his hired tutors educate him.

Transition from mental analysis to etudes

To have the right to make an etude, the previously mentioned type of detailed awareness needs to be carried out in a large number of episodes, each of which has its own conflicts, its own topics, and its own train of thought and actions, and each of which needs to be defined and taken apart.

Proceeding by fragments

Yet this kind of detailed analysis should not cover too much of the play's text at once; otherwise, the actor will not be able to remember it. For a start, we take a fragment, and with this fragment, the actor goes on stage to make an etude.

The size of the fragment can vary. It depends on the complexity of the play, the complexity of the episode, and whether the actors do not understand something or, on the other hand, whether they have easily and productively mastered the material. When commencing an etude, it is important that to a certain extent the actor has finished analyzing the fragment where a specific event or turn of action has been finalized.

In his analysis of the crowd scene in the first act of *Othello*, Stanislavsky provides a vivid example of a fragment worked to the point where the actor can commence an etude at full strength. [Listing a number of possible actions for the characters to perform in the Act 1 crowd scene, he suggests:]

To understand what occurred while half-asleep. To find out what somebody plainly does not know. To ask each other, to object, argue, if the answers do not satisfy, to make observations, to agree with them, to check or prove what is baseless.

To hear the shouts outside, to look through the windows, to look and to understand what is going on. You will not find a place for yourself at once. To attain it. To consider and catch what the nighttime rowdies are shouting. Who are they? You argue, as some are taken for others. They recognize Roderigo. To listen and try to understand what he is shouting about. You will not believe right away that Desdemona could decide on such a mad act. To prove some other motive, that it is either an intrigue or drunken nonsense. To swear at the rowdies because they do not go back to sleep. To threaten and pursue. Gradually, to be convinced that they are telling the truth. To exchange first impressions with neighbors. To express reproach or regret concerning what happened. Hatred, damnations and threats to the Moor. To find out what to do and how to proceed further. To consider every possible way out. To defend, to criticize or approve strangers. To try to learn the opinions of the leaders. To support Brabantio in his conversation with the rowdies. To incite to revenge. To listen to an order about pursuit. To rush to accomplish sooner.[2]

In this fragment, which has been brilliantly developed by Stanislavsky in his directing notes for *Othello,* he talks about a crowd scene in which the tasks and actions of the participants are collected in a comprehensive list, but this does not change the essence of the issue under discussion here.

There is no doubt that if a given fragment is developed with a similarly detailed knowledge of everything put into it – from external action to serious internal motives – the actor rehearsing the etude will not depart too far from the play because it will precisely *be* the play. He will have an episode of the play to study and master in terms of action by putting himself in the given circumstances of a role. He has already gotten into the play intellectually scores of times on one or another occasion, sorting out its text, reading one or another scene, checking himself, and affirming the correctness of his thoughts.

Having scarcely stepped onto the stage, however, once again a number of questions appear for the actor, questions he needs to solve correctly right there in order to make the etude. In what conditions does the action take place? Summer or winter, cold or hot? What time of day? How should the characters be dressed? Where do they come from, what is in their hands, were they tired or full of cheerfulness and energy? How do the characters behave: do they lie down, walk from room to room, or do they read or write or make something?

In other words, the first etude rehearsal immediately pushes the actor into all the details of the event's physical life. As soon as he tries to put himself in the given circumstances, he immediately acquires a more complex awareness of the event, and his internal and psychological state become inseparable from his physical and emotional state.

Of course, the actor encountered all these questions earlier, in the former rehearsal method, but only in the later stages of rehearsal. During the lengthy table period [of the earlier rehearsal method], the physical side of life was only assumed, instead of being shown how it develops, as in an etude. It is impossible to overstate how invaluable a service this unity renders for the actor, since, in the stress-free conditions of an etude, he imperceptibly comprehends what was formerly achieved only after many days of table work.

It is one thing to understand the feelings of Mercutio and Tybalt during their duel, and absolutely another to actually perform this duel.

One thing to reflect about the drinking spree of Sir Toby and his friends in *Twelfth Night*, and another to participate in it directly.

Episodes that seem difficult to assimilate suddenly become accessible and clear when they become part of the ordinary psychophysical life of the actor and are perceived, as Stanislavsky said, not only with the mind but also with the entire creative organism.

Approximating the production values

Which is why, when moving on to etudes, we try to ensure that the stage space intended for work looks approximately as it should in performance. If people eat and drink in the play, everything necessary to set the table properly should be there. If a guitar is necessary during the course of the action, then the guitar should be available at the first rehearsal. The music might not be written yet, but if so, then the actor can sing something of his own, but he certainly must play and sing. If the action occurs in historic times, the women should rehearse in long skirts and the men in cloaks or dress coats pulled from the costume inventory.

All this leads us to related directorial questions about locale. From a number of descriptions, we know that Stanislavsky suggested etudes for actors to imagine the locale and its associated conditions. Nikolai Gorchakov wonderfully described the etude work on a performance of *Woe from Wit*, when the rehearsal participants situated the furniture in Famusov's house in keeping with their own understanding, thus entering into the atmosphere of a historic Moscow mansion.[3]

Etudes of this kind were not intended to involve the actors in the scenic design decisions of a performance. I do not remember that Stanislavsky ever relied on the experience the actors acquired in etudes for determining the locale or overall scenic design for a play.

The locale is one of the major elements included in the director's plan. It reveals what the director seeks to create with the performance. Selected by chance or inaccurately, it can immediately shift the performance to a different key, introduce unfamiliar and inessential motives, and destroy the intended atmosphere. That is why the fate of each performance depends so much on the relationship between the director and the designer, on their general enthusiasm for the play, and on their ability to see it in identical ways.

It is well known that for the 'wedding scene' from Beaumarchais's comedy *The Marriage of Figaro*, Stanislavsky returned the rendering three times to such an outstanding designer as Alexander Golovin, since he did not correctly understand Stanislavsky's plan.[4] And then, instead of the traditional scenic grandeur, there was the by now well-known courtyard – a small simple space encircled by three tile roofs and with a colour spectrum comprising a dark blue sky and white walls illuminated by the hot southern sun. It was important for the meaning of the performance that here, in the *backyard* of the count's estate, simple people held their own celebration and rejoiced in the marriage of Figaro and Susan.

In the traditional practice of Russian theatre, the work of the director with the designer usually precedes the beginning of the rehearsal period, and this circumstance alone already refutes the idle talk about the director having the right to prepare a performance only together with the actors.

My personal experience convinces me that accurate prearrangement of the locale facilitates etude work. Going into the first etude, the actor immediately gets into the conditions of a space that should be made livable for him in the course of all later work.

Post-etude analysis

So, now the stage is arranged, all the accessories are in place, the actors have put on roughly accurate costumes, and the first etude rehearsal begins. It will not necessarily proceed directly without a hitch. I repeat, to create an etude is not a simple task, even if it is well prepared during the period of 'mental analysis'. When the actor enters the rehearsal space, it is necessary for him to overcome a particularly noticeable constraint, a well-known mental block: he thinks, 'What is next?' He is afraid of missing something and, of course, at the beginning he does miss things, taking only what he managed to understand organically and what remained in his memory better or most strongly.

A scene that was rather long in the play itself sometimes appears quite scanty in an etude. Its motivation looks weaker and more primitive than that provided by the author. The reasoning of the actor is weaker than his role in the text. Moreover, it is immediately clear exactly what the actor missed, what he did not understand, what we planned with insufficient accuracy during the period of 'mental analysis', and where we deviated from the essence of the play. It is clear not only to the director in the role of mirror for the actor, but more important, it is clear to the actor as soon as he takes the play script back in his hands. That is why immediately after the etude is done, the actor returns to the table again for continued analysis of the scene just played.

It is essential to plan rehearsals so that etudes always alternate with their analyses at the table. It is very important that the actor does not break away from the play script even for one rehearsal, and that he can check everything he planned for the etude right there.

In *An Actor's Work on a Role*, Stanislavsky advises the students who had just analyzed the initial scene of *The Inspector General* to make two lists. One list containing the actions they just performed improvisationally and the other containing the actions specified by the author. Then compare both lists to 'strengthen the moments of difference.'[5]

Here 'checking the lists' occurred after post-etude analysis. This is not quite the same 'mental analysis' that the actors undertook prior to the beginning of etudes. The actor has already shifted to the period of physical embodiment, felt himself in his character's position, and tried to perform from within his own identity. He returns to the table excited and energized by the experience of analysis in action that has just taken place, and consequently he carefully identifies his omissions, mistakes, and the shallowness or superficial understanding of this or that circumstance of the play. Right there he reads the text again. Right there he grasps the author's wording, and he recognizes it happily. (How much better, more precise, and more significant the text is than he, the actor, could express with his own words!) The omissions lead to disappointment, and a desire arises in the actor to go on stage and rehearse again. Furthermore, this creativity is captured, as Stanislavsky said, in the heat of the moment instead of coldly at some distance in time.

In the period of etudes and their subsequent table analyses, the circle of questions expands amazingly, questions both for the actors themselves and for the director, and questions that arise concretely, from 'inside' the role. Questions the actors must ask, otherwise it will be difficult for them to function in the next etude and they will not be able to get to the end correctly in the given circumstances of the play.

'To enter a scene properly, instead of like an "actor," you need to learn who you are, what happened to you, where you live and in what conditions, how you spend the day, where you came from, and a lot of other given circumstances you have not created yet, but which influence your actions. In other words, to simply step on stage correctly, it is necessary to be informed about the life of the play and your relations to it', as Stanislavsky explained the essence of his method to his students.[6] In the studio, we young directors needed to observe how questions actively arise from the actors every time a play was rehearsed with the etude method. By being placed in conditions where it was necessary to express the author's thought in their own words, the actors greedily absorbed everything that helped them to understand the character's behaviour and thinking.

In our production of *The Bourgeois Gentleman*, we began with a scholarly lecture about Moliere's theatre and the culture of Moliere's era. The lecture was listened to with interest, but questions for the lecturer came only from the director. The actors did not pose any questions of their own. But after a little time had passed, and we had started to rehearse the play according to etudes, at that point the actors literally showered the scholar with the most various kinds of questions.

What education did the middle class receive during that time in France? Were the merchants able to read and write, or is Jordain an exception in this sense? Is it true that women of the world went outdoors in masks or covered their face with fans? What is a *pistole* and a *Louis d'or*, and what is the present worth of these coins? Did they keep money in sacks or in purses? Who poured wine for the ladies at the table, the gentlemen sitting next to them or the servants standing behind the gentlemen? What did a middle-class woman engage herself with at that time? Did she help her husband, trade at the shops, or manage the household? Did they sniff tobacco then? Whose prerogative was use of the staff? Did middle-class or upper-class persons walk with it? And many other things.

Among these questions was much the scholar had mentioned in his introductory lecture, but at that time these facts had not yet become requirements and consequently slipped out of our memory straightaway. Now the actors perceived them as a direct practical need.

The same thing happened at the Yermolova Theatre when we rehearsed *As You Like It,* a performance in which Active Analysis formed the basis of rehearsals. I remember how insistently the actors interrogated a scholar about Shakespearean theatre, the role of the clowns in relation to the crowd in the pit, their origins and education, whether they are simple people or members of the nobility, and what compels them to go into this craft. We learned about the Forest of Arden, read and consulted resources. In general, the educational curiosity of the actors in this performance was very high, but it emerged from etudes.

Acquaintance with nature, with the living prototypes of the play, excursions to places where an action occurred, visits to museums, exhibitions, art galleries, study of the material culture of an era – everything that can facilitate the actor's penetration into the essence of a character – none of this is ignored in the new method. On the contrary, the requirement for such knowledge becomes more active in the course of the etude because the actor himself looks for concrete material to help him get into this or that circumstance of the play. He looks for it himself because he understands that without this knowledge he cannot move forward and get closer to the character.

So, from etude to etude, the actor introduces everything more deeply into the living atmosphere of the play, gropes for bridges from himself to the character, and learns his inner world. In each of the succeeding etudes, he acts with an increased richness of motivations and with a stronger personal feeling about the events in the play.

The goal of the etude is reached when the actor has not only given substance to the facts of the play, correctly evaluated them, and understood their sense and value for the fate of the character but also managed to justify them creatively. Then he can act productively and efficiently in the circumstances given by the playwright, and the improvised text will be able to arise in him organically.

By checking the finished etude of the play and then coming back to the author's text, the actors are assured not only that the author's idea has been correctly understood and reproduced in the etude but they also imperceptibly acquire some part of the text for themselves organically. It also happens that by repeating etudes, the performers already begin to make use of the author's vocabulary to some degree.

Post-etude transition to the table and the appeal to the author's text provide an opportunity for the actor to check himself and to understand both the mistakes and the correct progress of a role. In addition, if he made the etude correctly, the actor perceives the author's text with great creative pleasure because he correctly transferred all the author's thoughts into action and verbal expression. At this point, a genuine creative bond takes place between the actor and the author, and this provides a special pleasure that will bear additional scenic results.

Managing mistakes in etudes

Undoubtedly, mistakes occur in the course of etude rehearsals, and quite frequently. They are mainly caused by the chain of logical events acquired imperfectly from the author's plan, from his thoughts, and from the implications of the play.

I can provide an example from my own practice. We were rehearsing Pushkin's poem, 'The Gypsies', with students from GITIS.[7] The entire poem had been analyzed in detail, and we performed some etudes. We reached the point of Zemfira's secret rendezvous with the young Gipsy. The etude went well. Emotionally, the events were live and organic. The students who were not involved with this particular piece praised their companions. It was especially satisfying that the student rehearsing the young Gipsy – who wanted to rescue his lover and give her a chance to run away from the anger of her husband – carefully approached Aleko [her husband] and exposed his breast to the blow of the knife. He decided to sacrifice himself if only Zemfira could remain alive. Aleko sticks the knife into him, and when Zemfira rushed to protect her lover, he kills her as well.

On the whole, this was correct. The sequence of events was taken into account, the logic of the actions appeared to be true, and the feelings were live and real.

Long ago, no matter how successful the etude was, I developed the habit of sitting down at the table immediately afterward to check whether the etude was on course with the author's text. And this time we did not change our rule. According to Pushkin, the Gipsy does not want to rescue Zemfira, but Zemfira wants to rescue the young Gipsy. In the etude, the student playing the Gipsy was excited, perhaps, and performed very striking representations, but they did not proceed from the author's plan accurately. Nevertheless, in this case, comparison of the etude to the text of the poem indicated that the author's text was easily and organically remembered by the students, and when the etude was repeated all the actions were executed according to Pushkin's plan. Etude verification with the text provided an opportunity for deeper penetration into the behaviour of the characters and into the author's exact vocabulary, and thereby into the genre of the work.

Moving to the next fragment

How many times is it necessary to rehearse a scene according to etudes? As soon as the actors are close to the words of the text and the content of the scene becomes clear, the need for the etude disappears, and then it is possible to move on to the following fragment. No fixing and polishing of etudes is required. If the actors gain too strong a footing with their own text, they will remember it and immediately become comfortable with it even though it is foreign to the author's text. Consequently, the etude rehearsal will lose meaning. The director should watch closely so this does not happen.

The creation of a characterization is a long and difficult process, and further ahead the actor will identify and deepen many things in the later stages of his work on the play. On the other hand, it is natural that in etudes he will not achieve the wealth of thought the author's text provides for him. Nonetheless, thanks to a deep understanding of all the internal paths that give rise to the character's words, he will be prepared to comprehend the author's vocabulary. Etudes really help with this preparation.

In the course of Active Analysis, the actor is placed in a creative atmosphere by necessity (because it is not possible to make an etude without creativity), and he approaches the embodiment of a live person on stage more organically. Accordingly, the process of mastering the material of a role never becomes formal even for a minute and never bears a mechanical element within itself.

3

Main Advantages of Active Analysis

What are the main advantages of Active Analysis? Why did Stanislavsky try to introduce this method so insistently?

Responsibility of the actor

To begin with, the new rehearsal method markedly increases the responsibility of the actor, while at the same time fostering the creativity of the participants as a group. If the actor does not treat the period of 'mental analysis' seriously from the outset, he will not properly understand all the richness of the motives distinguishing his character's behaviour. He will not capture all the outcomes, all the turns of action, and he will be unable to perform in the etude organically. After all, he has no text behind which to hide his helplessness – he needs to create the text for himself. Without capturing the material of the role in the course of 'mental analysis', he will be unable to improvise in the etude, unable to participate in the general work, and will let his companions down and disrupt the etude. This feeling of shared responsibility for rehearsal – since its effectiveness very much unites the company – creates that special working atmosphere that is so necessary for creativity.

The actor in an etude has to be focused. As in life, if the process of his existence in the circumstances of a role does not develop if he ceases to think, listen, and evaluate the sequence and logic of his actions even for an instant, then he will inevitably miss the thread of the events and be unable to find the correct actions or the necessary words.

Etudes are full of surprises for their participants. It is never possible to foresee a partner's words in advance. The actor in an etude does not simply wait for the next remark from the actors standing around him. Instead, he perceives the emerging thought directly. Absent-mindedness, lack of concentration, and merely formal participation by an actor gives a more painful account of itself in an etude than it does at table readings, more painful because it is more obvious. Etude rehearsals, as a rule, develop 'in the nerves', and creative work emerges on its own, with little special effort from the director.

The creativity of the actor

Throughout Active Analysis, one consoling thought nests in the subconscious of the actor: 'We are only doing an etude!' The actor knows very well that the etude is simply a path from himself to the character, and that the characterization as such is still far off. Awareness that an etude is only a rough draft makes the actor courageous. A mistake in an etude is not so bad. The etude is a test, a search and a check. It is an approach to the creation of a role. The etude is a draft copy, which exists precisely so there are no 'blank pages' in the work of the actor, no empty, inexpressive moments. In an etude, nothing is fixed 'permanently' and nothing is done for the last time.

This awareness – 'We are only doing an etude!' – removes the psychological constraints from the actor, thereby liberating and empowering him. He willingly tries and easily discards from what was just found. His imagination works actively and sharply. He is improvisationally in shape, not only for the period of etude rehearsals but also for the entire period of work on the play. It often happens that in the late stages of rehearsal the actors begin to argue or disagree on some point, and then somebody unfailingly says, 'Well, let's do an etude!' They go on stage and check the episode that is not clear, switching easily into improvisation even after learning the author's text.

Scores of times when observing this surprising 'liberation' of the actor in an etude, one involuntarily thinks that even if the etude method had no other advantages than this wonderful 'liberation' of the actor, we should make Active Analysis a part of our daily regimen in the theatre.

'Me in the given circumstances'

The preceding advantages of the new technique are far from the only ones. Is it not important, for example, that by plunging the actor into the given circumstances of a role from the very beginning of work, etudes force him to work not intellectually but concretely 'from himself' in situations from the play?

Naturally, when actors undertake an etude rehearsal for the first scene of a play, the huge work of merging the internal and external elements of a role still lies ahead for them. Even then, the actors will not ask the director about a role in the 'third person', because the 'first person' is already automatic ('Am *I* acting correctly here?' 'Do *I* have the correct train of thought?' 'What does this fact mean for *me*?'). Transition to the situation of the actor-character, 'getting into the character's skin', is wonderfully facilitated in etude work by the fact that the actor rapidly accumulates a personal, concrete existence in the given circumstances of a role. He carries out the actions of the character, thinks his thoughts and plunges into the nature of his feelings.

Thus, it is extremely important that etudes by definition assist the actor to maintain the correct sequence of all the elements of his internal life. By means of action, he is led towards the entire expressive world of the characters' spiritual and physical life.

How does this happen? We already said that etudes and preliminary analysis of the play at the table offer a way to push the actor towards the character's line of actions more quickly, forcing him accurately to answer the question: 'What do I do in this episode?' Let us assume we are rehearsing Ostrovsky's play *The Snow Maiden.*'[1] This is one of his finest plays, but the beauty and complexity of its vocabulary often lead to the collapse of its effective structure. We will take for an example one of the monologues of the Snow Maiden herself. The Snow Maiden asks Mother Spring to grant her the emotion of love, which is still unknown to her. A big monologue, beautiful words, and it is easy to lose the line of action in it.

Ostrovsky writes that the Snow Maiden feels sad; she wants to love, but does not know the words. The emotion does not exist in her heart. She hardly begins to embrace someone when immediately she hears inside herself the 'name-calling, taunts, and pangs of childhood shyness behind her cold heart'. She can only *talk* about jealousy, which she learned without even knowing about love. Only *talk* about her envy of those who can love, about her tears, and her sleepless and painful nights . . .

I often saw young actresses and students become confused with the author's verbosity, as in a dense forest, and plunge unthinkingly into a generalized feeling of approval for the heroine. Rehearsing with etudes, without knowing the author's text yet, the actress realizes first of all that her action consists of convincing Mother Spring of her right to love, a right given by nature to every young woman.

However, having defined the action in this monologue, the actress cannot depend on this knowledge alone. Abstract action independent from given circumstances does not exist in nature. It is necessary to reject decisively the primitive idea that abstract logic can mechanically, by itself, lead the actor to his character, as though it were enough just to grasp this logic and the characterization will immediately be equipped for performance. If we identify the action first, it is only in order to move from its bare essence to all the specific motives that nourish it.

What does it mean in this case to convince Mother-Spring to grant the emotion of love to the Snow Maiden? Obviously and first, to convince her that without this gift she cannot go on living, that is, without knowing love. The performer should use her imagination to create a whole chain of images in order to plunge into the Snow Maiden's inner world. She needs to understand why she became troubled when a certain character abandoned her, for example, and another character confused her. Without understanding all this, all these given circumstances, she cannot perform the intended action accurately.

Let us look at another example. In a number of plays, whole episodes are constructed so that a character is waiting for something. Generally in these episodes the only abstract basis of action is – waiting. However, this action can appear quite differently as soon as we go into the concrete given circumstances, the nature of this character, and his internal life at a given moment. A military officer sent to the front lines waits for the woman he loves, and all his being is directed towards the time when he can return to her. Madame Ranevskaya waits for the auction to come to an end: will the cherry orchard be sold or rescued? A certain young woman painfully waits for the timid young man of her heart finally to say the words of love, a conversation that she prolongs in every way possible. In all these events, the characters are waiting for something in different ways! Consequently, from the action the actor immediately addresses the given circumstances nourishing this action, thus making it concrete.

Character

From the action *to* all the other elements of internal life – this is the path of the actor in the course of Active Analysis. Moreover, the first thing that emerges on this path is the character, that is, the identity of the person who executes a specific set of actions and displays particular behaviours.

Some theatre analysts are of the opinion that Stanislavsky's emphasis on action ignores the question of character as such. Comparison of Stanislavsky's final discoveries with his entire system, however, persuades us that, no matter which sphere of the actor's psycho-equipment held his attention at various periods of his life, he never lost track of the purpose his entire system serves – the creation of a concrete and uniquely human character on stage.

One time, when working on *The Inspector General*, Stanislavsky evaluated a finished etude. He called his students' attention to the fact that when he performed the role of Khlestakov in the etude himself, he ran like a shot into the room of the provincial hotel, quickly slammed the door behind him, and then peeked through the keyhole. In these actions he felt the essence of Gogol's character – a coward and a boaster, a small, vain person.[2]

Realizing one or another action in an etude, the actor immediately confronts the question of how this action personifies his character and what paths emerge that this character can and cannot undertake. During post-etude analysis, we can pause for a long time on what this character is capable of accepting and not accepting.

In GITIS's directing programme, we rehearsed one of the first scenes from Shakespeare's play, *Twelfth Night,* called 'Olivia's House'.

In the etude the student working on the role of Malvolio – who subsequently played it wonderfully – reacted with open anger to the jeers of Feste the clown. Returning to the table after the etude, we called the student's attention to the fact that such behaviour contradicts Malvolio's character and his ambitious plans. In another episode, Olivia says of Malvolio, 'Where is Malvolio? He is sad and civil, and suits well for a servant with my fortunes'. In the opinion of the countess, this means that Malvolio is completely different from how he appears to the servants who know him – to them, he is a rude, self-important fellow. This means that he is masquerading and playing a certain role in life. Accordingly, whenever he is near the countess, he will not for one moment give up the 'capital' he has acquired over many years of serving her.

Then we re-read everything that concerns Malvolio, including what the other characters say about him. At that point, the student began to understand that Malvolio behaves one way with the servants and absolutely another way with the countess. His double-faced existence is saturated with the false and sanctimonious morals of a Puritan. Knowing this about the character, about his social characteristics, about the thematic plan enclosed in the character by the author – knowing all this, we started preparing a small etude from a passage where Malvolio has almost no text. However, he appeared often enough in this short conversation that the student rehearsing Malvolio sharply changed his behaviour in the next etude. Without eliminating his internal reaction to Feste's jeers, he regained control of himself and tried to remain outwardly reserved so as not to lose his monumental tranquility, which is so characteristic of countess Olivia's 'sad and civil' butler.

The actor should perform an etude by starting from his own identity (italics added). This means he needs to analyze himself, the character-actor in the given circumstances of the play. But since these circumstances are not what formed the identity of the actor in real life, the gap between them can be found immediately. What the actor needs to relinquish, what he needs to overcome in himself, and what traits of his own life are suitable as 'construction material' for creation of the character – all this becomes clear to the actor.

Now a final example. The second-year students at the Shchepkin School-Studio,[3] though unquestionably still very young, nevertheless worked on Chekhov's one-act play, *On the High Road*.[4] In the play

Bortsov is a landowner, or rather a former landowner who is now a vagrant and an unfortunate, fallen person. His wife has left him, his house is derelict and has been sold at auction, and he has no money. Bortsov is now an anonymous and extremely pitiable person. There is only one 'holy relic' for him – a medallion with a portrait of the beloved wife who ruined him. There is no hope for Bortsov to recover and there are no more desires left for him except the constant painful desire to drown his grief in drink.

We discussed all this during the period of 'mental analysis'. When preparing the role of Bortsov, however, the student did not consider the character's biography or the circumstances behind his fate. Thus, at first he tried to portray only one of the character's actions in the etude – the aspiration to drink, to get hold of liquor he had no money for, and to cadge vodka from the owner of the tavern.

What happened? Bortsov immediately blended in with the crowd of tramps crowded together at the inn and lost any individuality. Actually, this is incorrect because Bortsov is neither pitiable nor anonymous. He does not abandon his background, his education, and those habits he acquired over the years – manners that are inseparable from a person who has developed within a certain environment. Bortsov in rags is fundamentally different from his companions in misfortune, just as the Baron in Gorky's play, *The Lower Depths*, differs from the other inhabitants of the flophouse. In our etude, this important social truth was overlooked.

Returning to the table after the etude and studying the play for an explanation of this failure, the student began to understand how Bortsov's vocabulary differs sharply from that of his current environment. For example, he and only he can utter lines such as 'You don't understand me. Understand me, you fool, if there's a drop of brain in your peasant's wooden head, that it isn't I who am asking you, but my insides, using the words you understand, that's what's asking! My illness is what's asking! Understand!'

The author's special language

At this point, we approach a very important feature of working on a play with the etude method, a feature we have said nothing about up to now. We have said previously that after rehearsing an episode with improvised text, the actor immediately goes to the table and re-reads the author's text, checking everything that just emerged in the etude. In these post-etude analyses, however, it is necessary to demand from the actors not only refinement of the etude consistent with its actions and topics but also scrupulous attention to the vocabulary and grammar of the character's speech.

This is important for two reasons. First, the dialogue of a talented writer is unique. It specifically addresses the personality of the character, the course of his thoughts, and his internal life. We try to help the actor understand why his character speaks a lot or a little in a given situation, for example, and why a pause or a monologue arises. If ellipses interrupt the character's speech, it is necessary to understand the psychological motives behind this element of speech. On the other hand, if the character speaks smoothly, effortlessly, and at length, where does this verbal freedom come from? Has the character expounded on the same subject scores of times during his life, and is that why his speech flows almost mechanically and without involving much feeling? Why, for example, does the teacher in *The Bourgeois Gentleman* philosophize as much as he does when he talks about physics and other sciences? Is it because the main character also understands these subjects and can talk about them for hours as well? Or is it ultimately because it is very important for the teacher to convince this other person, obtain his approval, and push him in a given direction? All this needs to be understood and resolved. Otherwise, the actor will not be able to grasp the logic of the action or the truthful behaviour of the character in the etude.

Apropos this point, Shakespeare's characters possess a type of speech that is infinitely rich, penetrated with images, bursting with live comparisons and forceful, inexhaustible arguments. This means that when approaching Shakespeare by means of etudes, it is necessary to acquire a similar response to life, to understand it and feel it; otherwise, the proper words will not emerge. To rehearse a poetic play with etudes, the actor needs to feel the genuine excitement that compels the author to place verse instead of prose in the mouths of the characters. And when this works, when the actor is really close to building a mental image of the character, expressive verse-type speech is often born involuntarily. It may be rough and naive, but all the same, in some way it will match the tone and scope of the author's own. This has happened with a number of students and actors who have worked on a role that uses poetic text.

The actor needs to grasp the text not formally but through all the richness of the internal contents put into it. Etudes pursue this goal as well – leading the actor to the system of thought-expression provided by the author. This means it is necessary to study this specific type of language and understand why the author needed to write this way and not some other way. In addition, if the author provides a monologue, the actor's improvisation should approach the form of a monologue, instead of being reduced to three scanty phrases that only transmit the author's thought schematically.

Studying the vocabulary of the play in post-etude analyses, the actor sees his mistakes as in a mirror, begins to understand where he expressed a thought inexactly or primitively, and where he erred against the author's poetry and overall style.

Critics of the etude method say that the actor is not a writer, and that he obviously cannot match the words provided by author's talent or the power of his thinking. That everything said by the actor in an etude will invariably be smaller and more poorly expressed than the play's original text. Why deliberately doom the actor to such vulgarization, they say. Is it not better to enrich his heart and brain immediately with the author's exact words?

In the beginning, of course, the author's words will invariably be foreign in the mouth of the actor and foreign to what is actually being created in his soul. Obviously, the actor is not Shakespeare. He cannot improvise in etudes at the level of a great literary artist, but he can and should create a world in himself that allows the characters to think, for example, in a Shakespearean way. And since the words in an etude emerge involuntarily from the actor's internal sense of the events, comparison of his words with the original text serves as a barometer of how far the actor's mastery of the author's thought has advanced. That is why after etude analyses the author's vocabulary can and should be discussed.

The second plan

But now we should return to the etude method's other advantages. We already found out that etudes offer the shortest route *from* the action *to* all the other elements of the internal life of the role, and most of all to the nature of the character. After talking about the character and encountering his specific paths in an etude, it is relatively easy to observe whether the actor has grasped all the manifestations of the character. Not least, the huge world that comprises the character's internal world, a world Nemirovich-Danchenko called the 'second plan'.[5]

Touching again on the student who rehearsed the role of Malvolio, from the first steps of Active Analysis it was necessary for him to face the fact that he could not perform a situation truthfully without understanding Malvolio's second plan. Ordinarily, an actor seldom plunges very deeply into the living concreteness of a scene, circumstance, or episode. Indeed, the events in themselves are always greater than the words spoken by any of the characters involved in them. The purpose of the etude additionally consists of opening this internal world and revealing the entire undercurrent of the play that nourishes the words. Practising Active Analysis for many years, I am convinced that with its help it is possible for actors to make a number of very difficult processes such as the second plan incomparably easier.

I remember how MAT actor Nikolai Khmelev adopted parts of the etude method for a production of *As You like It* when he became Artistic Director of Moscow's Yermolova Theatre. Instead of sitting around the table for a long time, he decided to do a run-through in which the actors spoke their own words, although the action, relationships, thoughts, given circumstances and everything else was still Shakespeare's. Khmelev expressly praised the acting of Jacques and Orlando because they performed so easily and energetically with each other and with a truly Shakespearean sense of comedy. It happened this way because the actors had been trained in etude work at GITIS. Since they were able to create the feeling of a creative portrayal for themselves, it came back to them again every time they played their scene together. Moreover, it did not desert them even when the actors employed the Shakespearean text. On the contrary, everything became brighter and more metaphorical, and the Shakespearean text was laid over the wonderfully developed nature of this relationship.

Internal monologue

Stanislavsky and Nemirovich-Danchenko were also engaged with the question of the internal monologue.[6] Both of them considered that the actor on stage, like anyone in life, always has unspoken words inside him. After all, what we say is only a small part of a never-ending stream of thoughts arising in a person's dialectical relationship with reality. Thus, an etude is impossible without an internal monologue.

I struggle with actors who do not believe what the internal monologue can achieve and who do not trust in the value of the second plan. They do not trust in them because of their prior experience with directors who consider these concepts 'bookish'. But genuine actors do not simply play separate objectives. On the contrary, they can bring the entire 'train' [inner life] of their role onto the stage. For me, this question is very important and relevant. I notice how actors decline when this form of inner life is taken away from them.

Etudes offer yet another advantage that enhances the process of communication via the internal monologue. Namely, the impossibility of knowing what will come from the partner and what words will expressly stand out. We have already said that during table rehearsal the actor often waits for the remarks of his partner, while in an etude he perceives his partner's thoughts directly. He only knows approximately how the scene will develop; today's nuances can be different from yesterday's, and tomorrow's different from today's.

Internal vision

It is possible to say the same thing about internal vision, another important element of Stanislavsky's system.[7] As an actor, Stanislavsky considered internal vision as a powerful means for preserving the life of a role. The 'film' of images, which Stanislavsky also called the 'illustrated subtext', gives the text the force of picturization and the force of a live impact on the partner as well as the viewer. Stanislavsky continually advised actors to 'Speak to the eye, instead of the ear of your partner'. In an etude, the actor confronts the need to develop such internal vision more quickly and graphically. In an etude, he cannot hide behind the text. His greatest need is to find the words for passionately convincing others, but he will not find them if he is unable to imagine specifically and visually what he wants to say and what he wants to achieve.

Stanislavsky expressed this remarkably in the directing journal for his production of *Othello,* where he speaks about the episode in which Othello tastes for the first time the poison of doubt that Iago pours into his soul: 'This monologue is interrupted, perhaps, by big pauses during which Othello frenziedly stands silently, examining a picture of what he is losing.'[8]

Such visions clarify what is unclear, bring closer what is far away, and make what is foreign personal, concrete and specific. This subject, as well as all the other subjects in Stanislavsky's system, do not go away, but are actively addressed during Active Analysis.

Characterization

I have already spoken about the fact that etudes allow the actor to feel the physical nature of a scene or an episode from the outset, while in lengthy table rehearsals this question is temporarily postponed.

In life, we make ordinary, daily, habitual actions automatically, without paying much attention to them. They are surrendered entirely to a person's internal life. However, on stage the actor is lost even when he needs to perform the simplest of physical actions unless he is trained in them. It is hard for an inexperienced actor to eat and talk on stage at the same time, for example, even though this kind of thing happens in life all the time. The preconditions of creativity, its public nature, sometimes complicate incredibly what had become a habitual reflex in life long ago. By forcing the actor from the very beginning of work to plunge concretely into the physical nature of a scene, the etude amazingly facilitates this process, imperceptibly leading the material aspect of the actor's on-stage existence to become a living habit.

Let us take, for example, such an important problem of the psychophysical life of a character as physical characterization.[9] If we do not quite become fully engaged in physical characterization, the result is generalized characters, bloodless, not identified by any individualized features [except those of the actor him/herself]. Alternatively, when the need for physical characterization is only remembered in the final stages of work and not organically acquired earlier, then a casual sort of external characterization is attached to the character merely as an external label.[10]

Stanislavsky and Nemirovich-Danchenko did not understand physical characterization this way. For them characterization was not only an outer form but also an integral part of the contents of a character. Stanislavsky argued that an actor can be recognized as a true artist when, out of a thousand human expressions, he takes what ideally addresses the entire psychophysical life of the character and expresses it. 'Characterization develops from how this person acts and thinks in these particular given circumstances.'[11]

And how a person acts and thinks in the given circumstances is precisely what is analyzed in an etude. Moreover, since the feelings of a character are more complex in an etude than during table rehearsals, in Active Analysis the actor encounters true external characterization more quickly and trains himself in it more actively. Thus, it is important to help the actors to see external characterization not only in terms of physical signs – walk, gesture, etc. – but most of all in the character's manner of communication, the nature of his perception, and how the character thinks and reacts to his surroundings. This is only a brief general statement about an issue that could be the subject of a separate work.

Tempo-rhythm

It is also necessary, at least in brief, to touch on the most difficult area of the actor's psycho-equipment, which Stanislavsky labelled tempo-rhythm.[12] It is clear that questions about this dialectic come before the actors in the first etude rehearsal, whereas earlier, sitting in quiet poses at the table, they only read about how their characters engage in duels, celebrate parties, or prepare for combats. In the old rehearsal method, tempo-rhythm only comes into play later on, when the actors are already stepping on stage and the [inevitable] mechanical race to speed up the tempo begins. This sometimes happens when the director reaches for the artificial intensification of a scene, without an organic basis and without a truthful inner life for the actors.

But if the actor reads the author's stage direction 'He runs in' before stepping on stage in an etude, he will not walk with a measured step anymore, but will certainly try to run. From the very beginning of work, he will get used to the feeling of this tempo-rhythm and be unable to rehearse any more without it.

In practice, most often actors do not encounter simple rhythms but complex ones in which a number of different motives overlap. We tried to explain this earlier using the example of Malvolio. In that etude, the complex feelings of the scene helped the actor to maintain a just proportion between the restrained tempo of his external life and the agitated rhythm of his internal life. Therefore, the concept of tempo-rhythm is naturally included in the process of the actor's existence in an etude.

Rehearsal productivity

Another strength of Stanislavsky's new method, I think, is the fact that it does not prolong the usual period for the preparation of plays, but, on the contrary, sharply reduces it compared with the customary time.[13] Our experience at [various theatres] showed that we would have been unable to deliver performances according to the assigned deadlines if we failed to inspire the *entire company* in the method of Active Analysis.

Alexander Griboyedov's classical comedy, *Woe from Wit* – an extremely difficult undertaking for the director and performers – was my first production at the Central Children's Theatre.[14] The situation became even more complicated when I ventured to work with unprepared actors using what was then a new rehearsal method for them. It was necessary to overcome both mistrust and lack of skill, along with the primary weak point of our work – communication between the director and the actors. But eventually the company was persuaded, believed in the force of the new method, and managed to analyze the entire play in etudes, except for the ballroom scene. Facing the ballroom scene, I retreated. I considered it too much to conduct such a large-scale etude, at least in the conditions given to us, and consequently the ballroom scene was directed traditionally, formally. The plan of exits and the behaviour of the guests and their reactions to the events were all precisely preplanned. The actors worked not from themselves, not from their own feelings of the action, and not from their own imaginations. A director's plan was given to them, and they simply tried to live up to it.

As a result, we fiddled around with the ballroom scene much longer than if the director had risked analyzing this scene with etudes in the first place. Moreover, the ballroom scene never did turn out the way we wished it to and thus became a subject of our constant concern. It needed to be cleaned up and continually re-rehearsed because the actors did not bring their own creative initiative to it from the outset. Consequently, it merely showed a group of more or less disciplined actors working according to someone else's will.

For intra-theatrical reasons, we had barely managed to carry out the etude work on Peter Yershov's play for children, *The Humpbacked Horse,* when the performance was postponed for a year.[15] When the following year we restarted the play – presumed dead because of its delayed production – the actors' memories of our preliminary work appeared so unexpectedly bright, and their knowledge of the play so deep and fresh, that we began almost at the same place we left off the previous year, just as though there was no long break. It is impossible to express how this circumstance inspired the actors, how quickly and amicably the work progressed – without internal doubts and without the usual slackening after a long period of inactivity.

Adaptations

This much is clear: by covering all the elements of internal life in their complex unity; by helping the actor to find both the internal, spiritual and external, material life of the actor-character; by arranging rehearsals to approximate those life situations in which a human being conceived by the actor can exist – by accomplishing all this, etudes very quickly and imperceptibly bring the actor to the threshold of the subconscious, that special threshold where, according to Stanislavsky, creativity begins. Etudes put the actor in situations where 'nature, released from constraint, will overcome the overly self-conscious nature of the actor's psycho-equipment'.[16] That is why with etudes the actor quickly acquires the adaptations [tactics, qualities] that give the diverse beauty of life to a work of art.[17]

In the finale of *The Bourgeois Gentleman* at the Central Children's Theatre, owing to the use of etudes, the turbans [of the 'Turkish potentates'] were removed and the masks covering the servants' faces were removed directly in front of a dumfounded Jordain. This ending was prepared consistent with our concept of the performance. We wanted to produce Moliere's play as a folk comedy, to show people laughing at the idle rich, a moral celebration of a folk truth, and the entire performance was guided in this direction. It concluded with the ending just described – organic for the play, yet emerging involuntarily through etudes from the actors' true feelings of the scene and its conceptual meaning.

Etudes also helped us to discover a solution for the love between Orlando and Rosalind (*As You Like It,* Yermolova Theatre), which the critics praised so much. If we judge from statements in the text, certain of the characters do not 'recognize' each other. Shakespeare's Rosalind, for example, does not re-appear in female dress until the last moment. Up to then, she continues to remain simply Ganymede, the lovely boy who agrees to 'play along' as the absent girlfriend of lovesick Orlando. Rehearsing in the usual way, without etudes, it is possible that the actress would get used to this situation and not be able to feel the convention of her disguise. But when our Rosalind changed into a man's clothes, hopped onto a tree for the first time, and clumsily imitated the habits of a naughty boy in an etude – she immediately felt the falseness of her situation and the impossibility of deceiving Orlando in such a state. Both the promptings of the heart and a thousand trifles would reveal the female in Rosalind, and she would be powerless to conceal her love. Furthermore, in the finale when she is 'recognized' by Orlando, she is 'recognized' not through words, but through intonations, gestures and looks. He 'recognized' her with all the feelings contained within that offhand term. He moved forward, trying to see that dear, familiar form previously hidden behind the guise of Ganymede. When it happened in an etude rehearsal, this event transformed all our further work on the performance. It formed the basis of their relationship as characters in a love game, allowing them to state their feelings under this masquerade more frankly and to feel the full-blooded Shakespearean emotional life of the characters more sharply. They caught the fancy of the audience as well.

I already spoke about the student who gave an exceptionally interesting portrayal of Malvolio in a performance of *Twelfth Night*. We were rehearsing the episode where Malvolio reads a note 'from the countess' believing he is alone, but the note was actually concocted and tossed to him by Sir Toby's cheerful band. Never before had I seen such temperament in this student. It was vanity convincingly inflated without mask or restraint. In less than five minutes, Malvolio grew to become the husband of the countess! From the exciting consciousness that 'I am to be the countess's husband!' he dived onto the floor, jumped around, sang, danced, and spoke entire monologues, not because he remembered them from the text, but because they emerged from the situation this person was placed in, just as in the play itself. There was such an abundance of magnificent, unexpected adaptations in all this that it was no longer necessary for the teachers to prompt him, but only to select or reject and provide a more judicious form to what he found.

To me, one of the qualities defining a truly modern performance is the accurate portrayal of scenes and roles. And a portrayal of this kind is organically connected with the nature and quality of its adaptations. Stanislavsky said that talent is expressed in the force, originality, surprise and variety of adaptations. As we know, he appreciated subconscious adaptations most of all, saying '. . . how they seize those being communicated with and are etched in the memory of observers! Their power lies in their surprise, courage and impudence'.[18]

Such is the good fortune of great talents. But it is impossible to wait for the moments when inspiration will arrive, and, as always, Stanislavsky looked for ways to awaken the actor's interest by searching consciously for adaptations. He warns about the risk of copying adaptations from outside (in particular, from the director), and explains how to make conscious adaptations 'familiar and sincere'. Speaking about conscious adaptations that the actor either receives from the director or thinks up for himself, Stanislavsky said: 'Animate them by means of psycho-equipment that will help you to pour a share of your subconscious into them.'[19]

I already spoke about the scene between Rosalind and Orlando, which created a whole chain of associated adaptations. Those were born subconsciously, but the director suggested others and persistently nurtured them in the actors. It seems to me the role of the director is significant here. Quite often actors reveal an interesting adaptation even in etudes. However, it often happens that neither the actor nor the director will pay much attention to it right away and will not consider there might be something valuable in it for the future. After a while, this adaptation will suddenly be remembered. Then it turns out to be important and essential.

I remember one situation like this. During the war, the Moscow Art Theatre produced Konstantin Simonov's play, *The Russian People*, and I was appointed one of the directors.[20] Somewhere near the approach of dress rehearsals, in one of the scenes the actor playing Globa took a piece of black bread, salted it slightly, and began to eat. Biting off piece after piece, he added some salt with intense concentration. The character talked about important things, about his life and that of his companions. The rhythm of his speech was slow, even restrained.

The movements of his hand sprinkling the salt were habitual, and his words were simply chilling. After rehearsal, I praised the actor for his discovery. 'I did not discover it', he said. 'You told me about it during the first conversation we had about my character. This stage direction was not in the play itself, and I forgot all about it, but recently I remembered it and considered how to find a place where Globa salts his bread, eats, and hides his excitement behind it.' This was true. The adaptation was prompted by the director and then forgotten, but at some point, it emerged from the actor's subconscious.

Here is another situation where an adaptation was born subconsciously in the actor, noticed by the director, and then nurtured and justified in the actor quite a long time before it became organic to his illustration of the role. I directed Ostrovsky's comedy, *Talents and Admirers*, at the Mayakovsky Theatre.[21] It was this leading actor's first role at a Moscow theatre. And he was working with etudes for the first time too. In the third act, the rich landowner, Velikatov, visits Domna, the mother of a provincial actress. He is bringing money for her daughter's benefit performance and gives Domna an expensive shawl as well. We outlined the action lightly. Velikatov needs to make an ally of the young actress's mother. He needs to impress her with the richness of his estate, the luxury of his house, a garden, an abundance of livestock, etc.

The actor was prepared for the etude. He clearly portrayed the fact that he had to bribe the mother to get to the young actress. For this task, as indeed for the entire role, willpower, resourcefulness and persistence are necessary. From their earlier acquaintance, Velikatov already knows about the mother's poverty and her love for economy and obsession with raising her own livestock. Both actors did the etude well. But besides the 'planned' action in the etude, something unexpected and interesting appeared. It was amusing to observe that a note of bitterness flashed in the landowner during the transfer of money, and that the mother responded to this sympathetically.

I began to insist on this adaptation. I was attracted by the fact that the actor-character of Velikatov was smart, powerful, and able to enjoy the process of a struggle that for the moment amused him. Moreover, that he looks for a way into the childishly naive heart of the mother, not only by offering his wealth but also his melancholy and loneliness, which is what the actress-character seemed to sympathize with in the etude.

But the actor resisted for a long time. It seemed to him that the text did not support this interpretation. I tried persistently to persuade him that this adaptation could provide unexpected psychological colouring to Velikatov's behaviour. Time passed and the actor finally believed in the idea, justified the adaptation, and now this scene is one of the best in the performance.

Style and genre

Interestingly, if an actor stays on track in an etude, through improvisation he often closely approaches the style of the author and even the very genre in which the author composed the play.

Twice I had to carry out an experimental demonstration of the etude method. One time was many years ago at the Yermolova Theatre, when we began work on *As You Like It*. The other time was at GITIS, when we prepared *The Merry Wives of Windsor*. Both were exceptions to the rule because etudes do not exist for demonstration purposes; they are an in-house rehearsal activity. I allowed this exception at GITIS because it was important to prove the feasibility of this method to the school's administrators to obtain their permission to work in this new way. We showed the entire play in etudes, in which nothing was fixed in advance, there were no established stage settings, and at the beginning of the demonstration I did not know how it would turn out.

The main thing that struck the viewers about this demonstration was the closeness of the actors' improvisations to the spirit and style of Shakespeare's play. One observer even refused to believe that these words and these aphorisms were not the author's text, and that the actors really improvised them from their etudes. The student playing Master Ford improvised as though he was actually overhearing Shakespeare's text, that is, the figurativeness of his speech was Shakespearean, and the temperament of a jealous man, his comic temperament, was genuinely Shakespearean. However, the student was still far from mastering the character, since we had only just begun working on the play.

The previous point is essential because it eliminates the false idea that by allowing freedom of improvisation, Active Analysis encourages the actor to ignore the author's style, which cultivates amateur work and haphazard form. Actually, it is just the opposite. Stanislavsky's new technique does not lead the actors away from the style of an era or the style of an author, but actively directs them towards it.

External form

The concept of external form is difficult to sort out. It develops from many directions, from an entire collection of efforts by the actors, the director, the designers and the composer. Style, which is the basis of external form, is expressed not merely in stage accessories and lifelike details, but primarily in human beings, in the nature of human relationships, and in the nature of the characters' inter-communication.

There is a distinct inevitability in how a personality is created by time, culture, education and environment – an inevitability that influences how he looks, moves, talks, thinks, feels and perceives the world. 'Style is the person himself' is a well-known aphorism.[22]

The external form of a performance arises, in essence, not when it is imposed on the actors by the director's authority, but when it emerges from the entire collective body of its creators. Both Stanislavsky and Nemirovich-Danchenko agreed on this question; the latter often said to his actors: 'The form should come from your own experiences and thoughts, instead of from mine.'[23]

In an etude, the actor cannot ignore the formal features of the play or its genre. In an etude, he enters into the very heart of an author's situation and tries to comprehend it. And since the content and form are inseparable in a work of art, a talented author represents not only living content but also content organized in a specific way and invested with a unique external form that is organic regarding this specific material.

In an etude, everything leads the actor towards the author's style, to the style of the era represented in the play, and towards its genuine inner life in terms of characterization and rhythm. By analyzing the characters in an etude and comprehending their mentality in line with a specific era, national sensibility and class affiliations, the actor unconsciously reflects all this throughout his entire life on stage.

Allow me to remind you, by the way, that in all post-etude analyses we fix the attention of the actors steadily on the ways in which the author arranges the intonations and how the personality of the character is reflected in the features of his speech. For after all, this is not only a conversation about content but also about the form of the play, its style, monologues, dialogues, rhythms of speech and many other questions no less important. In Active Analysis, discussions emerge early on about how the author writes about a character. Without knowing the vocabulary's features, it is impossible to learn the nature of the actor-character, but by studying these features in etudes, the actor comes closer to the vocabulary that is intrinsic to his character.

We often deal superficially with the question of style in the scenic interpretation of a play, that is, only formally, only in reference to its external signs. The clichés of 'Shakespearean' performance, with all their obligatory attributes – more than once ridiculed in the press – arise in this way. In Active Analysis, pointless discussions about style 'in general' never arise, only discussions connected with the specific features of the play. At the same time, by comprehending both the content and the form of the work in an etude, the actor develops a sense of style in himself organically and comes closer to the individual style of the author from the very beginning of work.

4

Beyond Etudes

In etudes, the actor's subconscious is awakened so that the borderline between analysis and embodiment is virtually eliminated. A time comes when the actor on stage is not yet fully characterized, but already he is not the person all of us know in life; a time, as Stanislavsky said [in response to this issue], '. . . where do you end and where does the role begin? You cannot take them apart.'[1]

Transition from etudes to rehearsal with the author's text

The question of the transition to rehearsals with the author's text continued to remain experimental for Stanislavsky up to his final days. He did not give us exact instructions in this respect. Therefore, this question remains experimental right up to the present. My own practice leads me to believe it is not necessary to construct an artificial boundary between etudes and rehearsals with the author's text. It would be hard to imagine a new rehearsal method whereby today there are etudes and tomorrow the actors will no longer be allowed to say any of their own words, but only the text of the author. No, the transition to rehearsals with the author's exact text usually occurs gradually, during the process of assimilation by the actors. Moreover, one scene can still be under development with etudes, while another is ready to go forward with the author's text. What is most valuable here is that this process usually proceeds almost imperceptibly for the actors.

The more carefully, more deeply, and in more detail, the actor analyzes the play, the more he learns the world of the play and its metaphorical system. And the more actively the etude approaches the play, the more direct coincidences will begin to appear between the actor's improvisations and the author's text. And once the actor finally seizes the entire huge world of associations in the play, he will inevitably realize that nothing expresses a given situation or thought so well as the author's original text. Studying the text in conditions like this is a joyful event for the actor, a mighty push on his way to comprehending the whole play.

Nevertheless, for this to happen it is also necessary for the author himself to be talented and to employ the exact wording necessary, so there are no gaps in his dramaturgical thinking. It often happens that when the actors begin to understand the living substance of a brand new play through etudes, they will prompt the author with a number of edits to help him replace empty words with those from the unique world determined by the facts of life in the play. Checking himself in etudes, the actor sensitively perceives the slightest inconsistency in the author's vocabulary, and, keenly defending his own tested experience, he not only shows a number of problems to the author, but also prompts him with accurate and interesting ideas.

Playwright Viktor Rozov knew what invaluable service etude verification of the text could provide the author, and during work on his new play, *Pages from Life,* he listened attentively to all the actors' remarks.[2] Furthermore, when there were disagreements about one line or another, he asked us to perform an etude to try it out. A similar form of 'working with the author' can be very helpful for a playwright while also helping the actor very much with transition to the play's text.

When the actor approaches the author's words in such a complex and deep manner, through the entire richness of their internal developments, the words remain effortlessly in his memory and his consciousness, they connect him with a number of associations, impressions and emotions. In addition, it turns out that the author's text contains the exact words the actor lacked to activate them logically, consecutively, productively and expediently.

Therefore, I personally do not see a period in Active Analysis that could be called the 'transition period' from improvisation to the author's text. Nevertheless, it is one of the questions posed most often. It seems to me this question arises if previous work was directed with insufficient precision or insufficient specificity. Alternatively, the actor may have been working satisfactorily during rehearsals, but was not studying his role outside of rehearsals. There are also situations when some of the actors have bad memories. Knowing this, the actor should naturally adjust his working process to avoid slowing down those who have already grasped the text. The etude method does not cure a bad memory; it only helps an actor to study a role in keeping with his imagination, thereby connecting words with actions by implication. After all, throughout the extent of etude analysis, the actor deals continuously with the play in itself. He studies his role in the process of 'mental analysis', comes back to it in post-etude analyses, re-reads the isolated places that have raised doubts and disagreements scores of times, and understands the play's verbal system and the nature of its language. By creating the illustrated implications of a role and accumulating internal visions, the actor is always verifying what he prepared alongside the author's text, attaching the pictures that have arisen in his imagination to various words of his role. Consequently, the internal visions the actor already acquired help to keep the author's exact text in his memory. Thus, the actor learns his role, learns it imperceptibly for himself, without mechanical tension and without the need for cramming.

Verification of the author's text

The director is responsible for one more task, namely, steering the actors towards unwavering verification of the author's text, including all the interjections and punctuation marks that define the nature of the author's intonations. The director cannot allow an 'approximate' vocabulary, verbal rubbish, or a tendency to be careless with the author's text. If such a tendency appears, it is necessary to stamp it out ruthlessly. However, this does not mean 'ad-libbing' happens more often in etude work or that it is more difficult to fight against than in the old rehearsal method. If the actor masters the text mechanically, without the participation of his consciousness, he can talk endlessly, easily adding unnecessary interjections, changing the word order of sentences, and adding other inadmissible rubbish that pollutes the author's speech.

In the course of etudes, the actor becomes accustomed to the text intelligently. Consequently, he never becomes indifferent to the text, to how a phrase sounds, why the author has an exclamation point here, or an additional epithet, or sounds an unexpected turn. He understands the reasons that compelled the author to organize the text in a particular way. This deep understanding of how the text of the playwright was born serves the actor as a subtle internal controller, signalling him about each deviation from the author's text and each of its smallest distortions.

Of course, this subject is not limited to the issue of accuracy alone. Work on the text in performance is not exhausted yet. It is a mistake to think that verifying the author's text means that everything about the text has been settled. Taken all together, Stanislavsky preserves the entire world of vocal technique in the etude method. Questions of rhythm, style, pauses, diction, clarity and beauty of sound, perspective in a monologue and the vitality of dialogue – all this continues to be the focus of our closest attention.

'The actor must be able to speak', Stanislavsky said many times, and this demands self-discipline, patience and training. We are continually engaged with all this at every stage of post-etude work, but further discussion of this particular subject lies outside the purpose of this article.

Production values and staging

Similarly, questions about production values and those connected with the staging of a performance are not part of our task here. We can only say that staging under the new method is essentially distinct from what the process was in former days, but unfortunately still persists at a number of theatres.[3]

Some directors prepare for rehearsal in a cocoon, developing a plan of the future performance at home, setting it down on paper first, and next day presenting the preplanned staging to the actors. Even if the director has talent, feels the specifics of the play perfectly, tries to consider the individuality of the actors, suggests organic ideas for the future performance – even then, staging [prepared in this way] is still divorced from the actors. This approach to staging negatively affects the future of the theatre and the future of the company's work as a whole because it suppresses the actor's taste for independence, generates passivity and lack of initiative, and prompts the same old questions to the director: 'Where do I move?' 'Where do I stand?' 'Where do I sit?'

With the etude method, the staging already emerges to a certain extent during Active Analysis. The actor involuntarily moves around the stage space according to the play's reality. The stage settings for an etude are not firmly established in advance, but they are not casual either. What creates them is the overall message and the entire complex of living expressions realized though the actors' imaginations. And if during etudes the actor comprehends elements of his internal state such as rhythm, characterization and the psychophysical actions of a character, this naturally pushes him towards the behaviours specified in the given circumstances.

At the same time, in post-etude analyses we deliberately focus the actor's attention on the staging that emerged in the etude. We force him to analyze what was truthful and what was incorrect or inorganic for his character and for his character's internal life at a given moment. Therefore, during etudes, various stagings begin to emerge that are quite often retained in performance.

This does not mean, however, that the staging that emerges through etudes can be mechanically transferred to the performance and left there. Certainly, the actors make valuable discoveries. More often, however, the huge work of selection and integration and replacement of inexact staging the actors may have found in their etudes, is still necessary for the director. Otherwise, there will be disorder, formlessness and lack of balance and harmonious movement. Otherwise, the staging returns to the power of chance, motley and illegible portrayals, and the elimination of artistic synthesis in the figurative system of performance. Moreover, this is one more argument in favour of the fact that the new method retains all the great complexity Stanislavsky established for our art.

5

Active Analysis Compared to the Method of Physical Actions

It only remains to bring up one more essential question. How does the Method of Active Analysis compare with the Method of Physical Actions?

Most everyone has recognized the inadequacy of the term 'physical actions', and most of all Stanislavsky himself, who used it with a number of more or less considerable reservations. Stanislavsky's reservations and the clarifications he included in the term are of considerable interest for us here as well.

The nature of Stanislavsky's reservations was always the same. In sum, they can be reduced to the fact that (1) physical actions should not be understood simplistically; (2) what is important are not physical actions as such, but the internal motives creating them; (3) there is a reciprocal linkage between 'the life of the human body' and 'the life of the human spirit'; and consequently, (4) physical actions should always be understood as *psychophysical*, as a unified expression of the actor-character creating them. 'In every physical action,' Stanislavsky writes, 'if it is not simply automatic but rather internal action, experience is animated from within, hidden.'[1]

There is one extremely important fact here. The fact that Stanislavsky uses the term 'physical actions' on two levels with two separate but related functions, associating it with two different stages of the creative process. When Stanislavsky speaks about the initial stage of preparation, about study and play analysis, he uses the term 'physical actions' in the sense of actions physically carried out, actually executed during the work of analysis. I, the actor, physically exist in the play. In this episode, I physically place myself in the position of the actor-character, and therefore 'I am' in the circumstances given by the author. From our point of view, this is what Stanislavsky meant by the term 'physical actions', at least for this period of rehearsal.

'If you not only imagine mentally but also execute physically the actions similar to those of the role and in the given circumstances similar to it, will you have an opportunity to understand and feel the original life of the person portrayed, not only rationally but also in the living feelings of the human body,'[2] Stanislavsky said. And these words are a direct justification for Active Analysis of the play and the role.

In the beginning, when the actor only studies and becomes familiar with the play and its physical actions, those actions that have been physically executed open the door slightly to the world of the subconscious, help the actor 'to knead the clay', and feel himself in the role. Then, after the actor has already created the role and grasped it, when the performance is ready, or work on it is close to completion, physical actions begin to serve another purpose. They become, as Stanislavsky said, a 'lure' for feelings, a kind of creative accumulator of feelings.

Naturally, physical actions are firmly connected with psychology. Dialectically speaking, communication inevitably involves one person with another, just as one reflex causes another, irrespective of the will and conscious creation. Beginning work on a performance with the 'score of physical tasks and actions', that is, fixing that actor's attention on the plain and simple 'life of the human body', the actor also involuntarily grasps the 'life of the human spirit'. This unity, this interdependence that allows the actor to begin with the simplest to achieve the most complex and leads the actor's whole organism into the given circumstances – this is what Stanislavsky considered a surprising discovery because it provides the actor with consistently creative energy, even beyond the one-hundred-and-fiftieth performance.

You are not in the mood to perform your assigned role in the performance today? You were tired all day, there was trouble at the theatre, your child is ill and it is difficult for you to concentrate? Well, in that case do not force your creative nature; do not demand the impossible from yourself. Try to carefully execute only one single simple action – you can certainly manage that – and it will become yours; and then the second after it, and the third, and the fourth – and once the feelings are felt and the awakened subconscious takes over, familiar feelings will begin to flood into your soul.

Regarding this process, Stanislavsky writes:

Your part, Leonidov [the actor playing Othello], is ready and it goes well. There is no need for me to explain the psychology and general line of the part to you; I should only tangle it up for you. My task is to help you to fix what has been done so far, to offer you a score so simple that you will be able to master it easily and follow it, without straying off to other lines which will tear you from your creative mood. This score, or general line which you should take must be simple; but this is not enough. It must be so simple as to surprise you. A complicated psychological line with all its subtleties and nuances will only muddle you. I have this simplest line of physical and elementary-psychological actions and tasks ready for you. So as not to scare away sentiment, let us call this line a *score of physical tasks and actions* and use it as such during the performance, but let us decide beforehand once and for all that the essence it contains does not, of course, lie with the physical task, but with the subtlest of psychologies, nine-tenths of which is composed of subconscious sensations. One cannot dig into the subconscious bag of human sentiments and rummage about in it as if it were your purse; the subconscious wants a different treatment, the way a hunter treats his prey, luring it from the deep wood into the open. You will not find the bird if you only look for it; you will need a hunter's decoy to attract it. It is just these decoys in the shape of physical and elementary physical actions and tasks that I want to supply you with.[3]

And further:

Can one assume that an actor who has prepared his part and the play, who has endowed every moment of the play with a whole poem of his imagination, who has experienced the illusion of its scenery and lighting in his mind, who is fully conscious of his make-up and costume, is in constant contact with other actors living in the same world and creating the same atmosphere and then, stimulated by the audience, reaches the highest fervor – can one imagine that such an actor, if given a task suitable to his situation on the stage, should remain cold in its performance?

Of course, everything is bound to come back to him, and the task will react as a decoy to the things which have accumulated unnoticed in the actor's soul, ready to break forth.[4]

That is why Stanislavsky appreciated the score of physical actions so much and insisted that every performer use it for every role, comparing it to a runway on which an airplane accelerates before lifting into the air, or a train track on which the passenger can travel to distant countries.

Everything is interesting and important in this discovery of Stanislavsky's; everything needs the most concentrated study and development. But in order for it to be of practical value in the theatre, it is necessary first of all to strictly differentiate when Stanislavsky speaks about the period of preparation and when he speaks about creative life in performance. In which sense is he using the term 'physical actions'?

Of course, we are talking about related concepts, a related group of phenomena based on a dialectical relationship between the physical and mental processes of a human being. But between the actions that have been physically executed during the initial analysis of a role, and the score of the elementary tasks in which the actor is in a role already finished, there are significant differences that cannot be overlooked.

If these differences are forgotten, for example, some actors and directors could end up believing that 'Stanislavsky said' it is possible to go on stage and by performing only the physical actions create a role without studying the play, without a plan, and without subordination to the author's thought. And that through the 'life of a human body' by itself, miraculously, the 'life of human spirit' of the role is created. Actually, according to Stanislavsky, physical actions can only serve as an accumulator of feelings, which in due time can be filled with feelings initially created in the closest connection with the psychology, temperament and inner world of the character, as when all this was expressed by itself.

6

Conclusion[1]

This article has been devoted to the new working method that Stanislavsky discovered in the final years of his life. The practice of my own work proved to me its great advantage and demonstrated the huge creative impulse included in it, which, as a result, facilitates the work of the actor on the role and the play.

Many opponents of this method take great pains to prove that Active Analysis is only an experiment that has been insufficiently confirmed in the theoretical and practical activities of Stanislavsky. It seems to me that we need not be frightened of the word 'experiment' if Stanislavsky's name is attached to it.

Moreover, the time has passed when Stanislavsky's thoughts were transmitted by word of mouth. Already an eight-volume edition of his works has been published.[2] Now anyone interested in the theoretical positions of the great director-scientist has an opportunity to study Stanislavsky's original statements in relation to one or another part of the system.

I would like to offer one of Stanislavsky's statements from his work on *Othello*, in which he defends the new method of work with absolute clarity. There Stanislavsky reminds his students about the process of work during which they used improvised text. He explains why he took the text of the play away from them at the beginning of work and forced them to speak the thoughts of the role in their own words. Stanislavsky reminds them that in the course of work he often prompted them with the sequence of the author's thoughts. He compelled actors to understand increasingly further the logical sequence established in Shakespeare's play. This sequence of thoughts became so necessary and habitual that the actor ceased to require prompting. Seeing the actors comprehend the line of tasks, actions and thoughts more deeply, Stanislavsky gradually started to prompt with Shakespeare's text, which was already becoming necessary for the actor to express the actions found in a role more completely. Only when the score of the role became clear did Stanislavsky allow them to learn the text.

> Only after this preparation [Stanislavsky writes] did we formally return you to the printed text of the play and your role. You did not have to cram the text because before long I took care to feed you, to prompt you with Shakespeare's words when they were necessary for you, when you looked for them and chose them for the verbal expression of one or another task. You seized them greedily, since the author's text was better than your own when you expressed a thought or performed an action. You remembered Shakespeare's words because you fell in love with them and they became necessary for you.
>
> What was the result? That someone else's words became your own. They were instilled in you in a natural way, without forcing, and therefore you did not lose the most important quality – verbal action. Now you do not simply speak the role, but you act with its words for the sake of expressing the main objectives of the play. This is exactly what we are given the author's text for.
>
> Now think, try to understand and tell me whether you believe that if you begin work on a role by cramming the text, which is what happens at all the theatres in the world in most cases, would you be able to reach the same result that is obtained by means of my technique?
>
> I will tell you in advance – No, by no means would you obtain the desired results. You would forcibly thrust the sounds of the words and phrases of the text into a mechanical memory of the language and into the muscles of speech articulation. Thus, in doing so the thoughts of a role dissolve and disappear, and the text would become separate from the tasks and actions.[3]

Our purpose here was to help readers to understand one of the most important parts of Stanislavsky's system and to explain his final discoveries, which provide new prospects for its application. We tried to show in concrete terms the practice of a new method of rehearsal through Active Analysis of the play and the role. At the same time, we would like readers to feel the deep connection of this method with all the fundamental provisions of the Stanislavsky System, which he approved and developed during an entire lifetime of productive activity.

The problems of action, to which Stanislavsky attached such great importance, the super-objective and through-action, the words (that is, verbal action, which Stanislavsky considered the primary form of action), internal vision, subtext, communication – all the links of a single creative process, the path to which is revealed organically in the process of Active Analysis. We cannot forget that in the creativity of the actor and the director, analysis passes into production by means that are elusive and complex. It is not always possible to catch the end of one process and the beginning of another, but that does not mean they are identical. The very selection of material needed to create the characterization and performance is a clear sign of the transition from analysis to production. This process and the working method described here come about organically, leading to a maximum of creative activity.

Responsibility and initiative for the creative organization of rehearsal according to Active Analysis lies, of course, with the director. Therefore, the director should master the methodology of the rehearsal process first. To be able to comprehend the genuine seed or the early stages of false work in the actors, to include time in the general work for the explorations of each individual – these and many other things are the responsibilities of the director.

But the most magnificent director becomes powerless if he does not satisfy the desire of all the participants to work creatively. And to work creatively means not only to be disciplined, attentive and serious, but also that the performer must work actively both at rehearsal and at home. This question of independent work with the etude method of rehearsal is of utmost importance. No matter how talented the director, there is an area in which he is powerless to help. The director cannot see for the actor, cannot think or feel for him. He can reveal to the actor the super-objective and given circumstances. He can be a reliable mirror reflecting the slightest falseness arising in the actor, but to live in a character, to be, to see, and to listen – this can only be done by the actor.

As soon as the actor ceases to live on stage consistent with a direct evaluation of the events; as soon as live internal visions, live communication and genuine psychophysical well-being are replaced by even the most magnificent characterization submitted to the director, the aroma of boredom immediately exudes from the stage. Without the living, original, passionate thoughts and feelings of the actor, everything on stage becomes dead.

Approaching the role by etudes in which the performer must imagine those circumstances, those internal visions, those thoughts he will subsequently speak about with the author's text – all this speeds up the independent work of the performer. The performer inevitably grows when facing the problem of independent preparatory work. He must accumulate internal visions to have the right to speak about them with his own words in an etude. He will gradually become fond of the more complex challenges of mastering the inner and outer world of the character's life. And he will come to appreciate the fact that independent work on a role consists of more than learning the lines by heart (as believed by some actors).

When you ask why Stanislavsky's system continuously developed, deepened and became such a powerful tool in modern Russian theatre, you will find the answer: because throughout his life Stanislavsky's primary philosophy was that to create real life on stage, you need to create according to the laws of life. To disclose the ideological intention of a character, to create a 'living person' on stage, to make use of the remarkable experience of the best masters of our art, and to treat the entire process with a sense of responsibility that can only lead to positive results – this is our common task.

Notes

Preface

1 For a perceptive summary of Efros's career written by someone who knew him and his work personally, see Anatoly Smeliansky, *The Russian Theatre after Stalin*, Tr. Patrick Miles (Cambridge: Cambridge University Press, 1999) 58–126.

2 See Part 2, 'Active Analysis Compared to the Method of Physical Actions' for Maria Knebel's explanation of the difference between the two methods.

3 JoAnne Akalaitis, Ingmar Bergman, Anne Bogart, Lee Breuer, Ping Chong, Liviu Ciulei, Martha Clarke, Richard Foreman, Elizabeth LeCompte, Des McAnuff, Katie Mitchell, Ariane Mnouchkine, Peter Sellars, Andrei Serban, Peter Stein, Giorgio Strehler, Robert Wilson – to cite only those virtuoso directors most familiar to English-language audiences.

Introduction

1 Much of the structure and tone of Part 1 draws from Anatoly Efros's early untranslated text, *Rabota Rezhissura nad Spektaklem* [the Director's Work on the Production], (Moskva: Tsyentralny Dom Tvorchyesky Rabotnikakh, 1960). Other writings of Efros that I relied on are cited in the text.

2 See Thomas in the Bibliography.

3 Maria Knebel, 'Vysokaya prostota' 46–49, also Maria Knebel, 'Superior Simplicity,' Sonia Moore, *Stanislavski Today: Commentaries on Konstantin Stanislavski* (American Center for Stanislavski Theatre, 1973) 44–47.

4 See Toporkov, passim.

5 Many influential actors, directors and teachers in the West have been allies of this faction, notably the members of the Group

Theatre (1932–1940) and their students and followers up to the present day.

6 Maria Knebel, *O dejstvennom analize p'esy i roli* (1959).

7 Maria Knebel, *O dejstvennom analize p'esy i roli* (1971).

Part 1, Chapter 1

1 For further discussion of the director-author relationship in the modern theatre, see Worthen.

Part 1, Chapter 2

1 This section draws from Tovstonogov, *The Profession of Director*, 144–154.

2 Qtd. in Warren 82.

Part 1, Chapter 3

1 Ref: '. . . plot must not be composed of irrational parts.' Aristotle 110.

Part 1, Chapter 4

1 Theatre for young audiences is a respected and integral part of the performing arts in Russia, where every city of any size has at least one theatre with such a mission. In addition to a professional staff of experienced actors and designers, some of the best young graduates of theatre conservatories are also selected to perform before these special audiences.

2 Qtd. in Zon iv. Translation © James Thomas 2015. Here and after this, all translations of Zon by permission.

3 Evgeny Vakhtangov (1881–1922), actor and director, member of the Second Studio of the Moscow Art Theatre, director of the Third Studio, which later become the Vakhtangov Theatre. Vakhtangov developed the concept of 'fantastic realism', which many analysts consider an ideal synthesis of Stanislavsky's ideas with those of Meyerhold.

4 Relaxation of the Muscles is a feature of Stanislavsky's system in its earliest iteration. See the eponymous chapter in *An Actor's Work: A Student's Diary.*

5 Stanislavsky is recalling his problematic experience with designer Gordon Craig's screens for a famous production of *Hamlet* at Moscow Art Theatre in 1911.

6 Vsevelod Meyerhold, Evgeny Vakhtangov and Alexander Tairov – all virtuoso directors – would have probably disagreed with Stanislavsky about this.

7 Known as the Studio on Povarskaya Street, this was a joint venture initiated by Stanislavsky and Meyerhold in 1905 to investigate the then-emerging style of symbolism. It folded after its first production both for financial reasons and because the actors were unequipped to perform satisfactorily in this new style.

8 Qtd. in Zon 459–463. Translation © James Thomas 2015. By permission.

Part 1, Chapter 5

1 Numbering throughout is based on the Folger Shakespeare Library Editions.

2 This section draws from the reading of Anatoly Efros, *Beyond Rehearsal*, 199–253.

3 Originally from *Eclogue X* by the Roman poet Virgil, and later from 1 Corinthians 13, as well as innumerable references from commerce, the arts and popular culture throughout history and up to the present day.

4 Op. Cit. *Beyond Rehearsal*, 199–253.

5 Peter Brook, 'Rough Theatre' in *The Empty Space,* 78–119.

6 *A Midsummer Night's Dream*, directed by Julie Taymor, Theatre for a New City, October 19, 2013 – January 12, 2014.

Part 1, Chapter 6

1 Opt. Cit. *Beyond Rehearsal*, 199–253.

2 Bernard Pomerance, *The Elephant Man* (New York: Grove Press, 1979). Based on the life of John Merrick, an unusually deformed and intelligent man who lived in London during the latter part of the nineteenth century.

3 *The Godfather*, dir. Francis Ford Coppola, writ. Mario Puzo, perf. Marlon Brando, Al Pacino, James Caan, Richard Castellano, Robert Duvall; Paramount, 1972.

4 See 'The Approach to a Role' in *An Actor's Work on a Role* [aka *Creating a Role*] 88–90. The great actor and teacher, Michael Chekhov, disagreed with Stanislavsky on this issue. In fact, the role of the imagination in the creation of character is one of the chief differences between their approaches to actor training. See Michael Chekhov, *Literaturnoe Nasledie* 337–338.

Part 2

1 Maria Knebel, *O dejstvennom analize p'esy i roli* (1971). Translation © James Thomas 2015.

Part 2, Chapter 1

1 See pp. 34–36.

2 See 'Director's Impression' in Part 1.

3 Knebel refers to the Soviet brand of formalism, which was used to label artistic work intended mainly for the development of the art itself rather than for the audience, or for performances employing complex and subtle techniques accessible only to the well informed.

4 Nemirovich-Danchenko 155–157.

5 Ivan Pavlov (1849–1936), Russian psychologist who established the basis for conditioned reflexes. For Pavlov's alleged influence on Stanislavsky, see Richard Hornby, *The End of Acting* (New York: Applause Books, 1996) 181.

6 Ivan Setchenov (1829–1905), Ivan Pavlov's precursor, who, it is said, bridged the divide between physiology and psychology.

7 Note the important distinction between Stanislavsky's approach to character development ('Me in the given circumstances') and that of Michael Chekhov ('Imaginary Body').

8 At the time Knebel's article originally appeared, Active Analysis had been around in Russia for over thirty-three years. And at the time of this book's writing, Active Analysis will have been around for over seventy-five years.

9 See 'Seed' in Part 1, Chapter 3.

10 Qtd. in Knebel (1971) 53.

11 See 'Opportunities for Etudes of Scenes Not in the Play' in Part 1, Chapters 5 and 6, passim.

12 Ibid.

13 See Director's Plan: Action Analysis, 29–42.

14 Qtd. in Knebel (1971) 55.

15 Ibid.

16 See 'Beginning, Middle, End' in Part 1.

17 See the eponymous section in Part 1

18 For a clear and insightful explanation of the concept of action and its central role in Stanislavsky' System, see Francis Ferguson, 'The Notion of Action,' *Tulane Drama Review* 9:1 (Autumn 1964) 85–87.

19 See the eponymous sections in Part 1.

20 The abstract talk of 'nation building' and 'citizenship' indicates that Knebel's students were probably working on Soviet social-realist plays, which would have been expected, if not required, in those times.

21 See the eponymous sections in Part 1

22 Qtd. in Knebel (1971) 58.

23 Second Plan is Nemirovich-Danchenko's term for the internal life of a character consistent with the play's main idea.

24 Qtd. in Knebel (1971) 61.

25 See 'framing event' in 'Thinking Eventfully' in Part 1, Chapter 3,

26 Ibid., 62.

27 Note the difference between the super-objective of the play and that of each character in the play, a distinction that is sometimes blurred in the writings of Stanislavsky and his followers. See the eponymous section in Part 1, Chapter 3.

28 The thread that the daughter of Minos and Pasiphaë gave Theseus to find his way out of the Minotaur's labyrinth.

29 I take this to mean that at the table the entire cast undertakes the process of mental analysis together, that is, without specific attention to their own roles as such.

Part 2, Chapter 2

1 See the eponymous chapter in Part 1.

2 Qtd. in Knebel (1971) 65–66. See also *Stanislavsky Produces Othello* 23–27.

3 See *An Actor's Work on a Role* 112–118.

4 For information about this storied production, see Margarita Chizhmak, 'The Creative Alliance of Golovin and Stanislavsky'. *Tretyakov Gallery Magazine* 44.2 (2014), www. tretyakovgallerymagazine.com/articles/3–2014–44/creative-alliance-golovinstanislavsky, accessed 2/3/2015.

5 See *An Actor's Work on a Role* 62–63.

6 Qtd. in Knebel 70.

7 *The Gypsies* (1827) by Alexander Pushkin. A married society woman falls in love with a Gipsy, and their affair comes to a violent end at the hands of her husband. The poem has been the source of several operas, as well as Prosper Mérimée's novella *Carmen*, on which George Bizet based his eponymous opera.

Part 2, Chapter 3

1 *The Snow Maiden* (1872) by Alexander Ostrovsky (1823–1886). The Snow Maiden asks her parents, Father Frost and Mother Spring, for their permission to live among human beings so that she can experience the joys of love.

2 See *An Actor's Work on a Role* 44–76.

3 The Shchepkin School-Studio is the conservatory wing of Moscow's Maly Theatre.

4 *On the High Road* (1884). Short story by Anton Chekhov. In a run-down village tavern in a remote Russian province, the ruined and betrayed landowner Semyon Bortsov is on a mission to track down his adulterous ex-wife.

5 See Part 2, Chapter 1, n. 22.

6 Internal Monologue is Nemirovich-Danchenko's term for a character's unspoken counterpoint to the spoken dialogue of other characters. In performance, it is generally suppressed; however, it can emerge openly through soliloquies and moments of direct confrontation. It is also commonly used as a studio exercise to check the accuracy and depth of an actor's assimilation of a character.

7 Internal Vision is Stanislavsky's term for a chain of imaginary pictures that enable an actor to 'see' the internal life of a character. Also called by Stanislavsky the Film of Images, Screen of Internal Vision and Illustrated Subtext.

8 Qtd. in Knebel (1971) 94. See also *Stanislavsky Produces Othello* 187.

9 The playwright creates a written character, while the actor creates a characterization, the psychophysical embodiment of character.

10 See the eponymous section in Part 1, Chapter 6.

11 Qtd. in Knebel (1971) 95.

12 Tempo-Rhythm is Stanislavsky's term for the dialectical relationship between a character's external behaviour and internal mood.

13 Virtually all theatres in Russia operate using a rotating repertory format, for which the complexities of scheduling usually require rehearsals to extend over a period of several months or longer.

14 *Woe from Wit* (1823) by Alexander Griboyedov (1795–1829). Classic Russian comedy of manners in verse.

15 *The Humpbacked Horse* (1834) by Peter Yershov (1815–1869). Classic Russian fairy tale.

16 Qtd. in Knebel (1971) 98.

17 Adaptations (adjustments, qualities, tactics) is Stanislavsky's term for the various ways in which the actor expresses the internal life of his/her character. See the eponymous chapter in *An Actor's Work: A Student's Diary.*

18 Qtd. in Knebel (1971) 100. See also the eponymous chapter in *An Actor's Work: A Student's Diary.*

19 Qtd. in Knebel (1971) 100.

20 *The Russian People* (1942) by Konstantin Simonov. Drama of Russian heroism in WWII.

21 *Talents and Admirers* (1881) by Alexander Ostrovsky. A comedy about actors and their admirers in a provincial Russian town.

22 Georges Louis Leclerc (1707–1788). '*Le style c'est l'homme même.*'

23 Qtd. in Knebel (1971) 103.

Part 2, Chapter 4

1 Ibid., 105. Also *An Actor's Work on a Role* 61.

2 *Pages from Life* (1953) by Viktor Rozov. A young woman, who is in search of happiness through her art, leaves her hometown and falls for a charmer who changes her life.

3 See 'Blocking' in Part 1, Chapter 6.

Part 2, Chapter 5

1 Qtd. in Knebel (1971) 110.

2 Ibid.

3 Ibid., 112. See *Stanislavsky Produces Othello* 183–184.

4 Ibid.

Part 2, Chapter 6

1 Knebel (1959) 116–118. Translation © James Thomas 2015.

2 Naturally Knebel refers to the 1952 Soviet-Russian edition of Stanislavsky's works, which was highly censored and abridged. An uncensored and unabridged eight-volume edition was published in 1988–1996.

3 Qtd. in Knebel (1971) 116.

Bibliography

Aristotle. (1961). *Poetics*. (F. Fergusson, Ed., & F. Fergusson, Trans.) New York: Hill and Wang.

Barba, E. (2009). *On Directing: Burning the House*. (J. Barba, Trans.) London: Routledge.

Carnicke, S. (2010). Stanislavsky and Politics: Active Analysis and the American Legacy of Soviet Oppression. In E. M. Renaud, *The Politics of American Actor Training* (pp. 15–30). New York: Routledge.

Carnicke, S. (2009). *Stanislavsky in Focus*. New York: Routledge.

Carnicke, S. (2010). The Knebel Technique: Active Analysis in Practice. In A. Hodge, *Actor Training* (pp. 99–116). New York: Routledge.

Chambers, D. (2014). Etudes in America: A Director's Memoir. *Stanislavsky Studies*, 4, 109–25.

Chekhov, M. (1995). *Mikhail Chekhov: Literaturnoe Nasledie (Michael Chekhov's Literary Heritage)*. (Vol. I). (M. Knebel, & N. Krymova, Eds.) Moscow: Iskusstvo.

Chizhmak, M. (2014, August 1). *Tretiakovskaia Galereia*. Retrieved October 6, 2014, from http://www.tretyakovgallerymagazine.com/articles/3–2014–44/creative-alliance-golovin-stanislavsky

Coger, L. I. (1967). Stanislavsky Changes His Mind. In E. Munk (Ed.), *Stanislavski and America: An Anthology from the Tulane Drama Review* (pp. 60–65). Greenwich, CT: Fawcett.

Efros, A. (2009). How I Taught Others. In A. Efros, *Beyond Rehearsal* (J. Thomas, Trans., pp. 199–254). New York: Peter Lang.

Efros, A. (1960). *Rabota Rezhissura nad Spektaklem (The Director's Work on the Production)*. Moscow: Central House of Creative Workers.

Efros, A. (2011 [2006]). *The Joy of Rehearsal*. (J. Thomas, Trans.) New York: Peter Lang.

Filshtinsky, V. (2013). Education through Etudes. *Stanislavski Studies* (2), 116–132.

Granville-Barker, H. (1974). Preface to *A Midsummer Night's Dream*. In H. Granville-Barker, *More Prefaces to Shakespeare* (pp. 94–134). Princeton, NJ: Princeton University Press.

Jackson, D. (2011). Twenty-First Century Russian Actor Training: Active
    Analysis in the UK. *Theatre, Dance and Performance Training, 2* (2),
    166–180.
Knebel, M. (1959). *O dejstvennom analize p'esy i roli (Active Analysis of
    the Play and the Role)*. Moscow: Iskusstvo.
Knebel, M. (1971). *O tom, chto kazhetsja osobenno vazhnym: Stat'i,
    ocherki, portrety (What Seems Especially Important: Articles, Essays,
    Portraits)*. Moscow: Iskusstvo.
Knebel, M. (1952). Vysokaya prostota (Elevated Simplicity). *Teatr*,
    pp. 46–49.
Kott, J. (1974). Titania and the Ass's Head. In J. Kott, *Shakespeare Our
    Contemporary* (pp. 213–236). New York: W. W. Norton.
Leach, R. (2003). *Stanislavsky and Meyerhold*. New York: Peter Lang.
Marowitz, C. (2000). *Recycling Shakespeare*. New York: Applause
    Books.
Merlin, B. (2001). *Beyond Stanislavsky: The Psycho-Physical Approach
    to Actor Training*. London: Routledge.
Merlin, B. (2004). *Konstantin Stanislavsky*. London: Routledge.
Miller, J. (1992). *The Afterlife of Plays*. San Diego: San Diego State
    University Press.
Montrose, L. (1996). The Imperial Votaress. In *The Purpose of Playing:
    Shakespeare and the Cultural Politics of the Elizabethan Theatre*
    (pp. 151–154, 158–161, 167–178). Chicago: University of Chicago
    Press.
Moore, S. (1967). The Method of Physical Actions. In E. Munk (Ed.),
    *Stanislavsky and America: An Anthology from the Tulane Drama
    Review* (pp. 73–76). Greenwich: Fawcett.
Nemirovich-Danchenko, V. (1968 (1936)). *My Life in the Russian Theatre*.
    (J. Cournos, Trans.) New York: Theatre Arts Books.
Nemirovich-Danchenko, V. (1984). *O tvorchyestvo aktyera (The Actor's
    Creativity)*. Moscow: Iskusstvo.
Pennington, M. (2005). *A Midsummer Night's Dream: A User's Guide*.
    London: Nick Hern Books.
Pitches, J. (2009). *Science and the Stanislavsky Tradition of Acting*.
    London: Routledge.
Smeliansky, A. (1999). *The Russian Theatre after Stalin*. (P. Miles, Trans.)
    Cambridge: Cambridge University Press.
Stanislavsky, K. (2010). *An Actor's Work on a Role*. (J. Benedetti, Trans.)
    New York: Routledge.
Stanislavsky, K. (2008). *An Actor's Work: A Student's Diary*. (J.
    Benedetti, Trans.) New York: Routledge.
Stanislavsky, K. (1961). *Creating a Role*. (E. R. Hapgood, Ed., &
    E. R. Hapgood, Trans.) New York: Theatre Arts.
Stanislavsky, K. (1948). *Stanislavski Produces Othello*. New York: Theatre
    Arts Books.

Tcherkasski, S. (2013). The System Becomes the Method: Stanislavsky – Boleslavsky – Strasberg. *Stanislavski Studies* (3), 97–120.

Thomas, J. (2013). *Script Analysis for Actors, Directors, and Designers* (5th ed.). New York: Focal Press.

Toporkov, V. (2014). *Stanislavsky in Rehearsal*. (J. Benedetti, Trans.) New York: Bloomsbury Methuen Drama.

Tovstonogov, G. (1972). Method. In *The Profession of Stage Director* (B. Bean, Trans., pp. 237–251). Moscow: Progress Publishers.

Warren, C. (1985). *T.S. Eliot on Shakespeare*. Ann Arbor, MI: UMI Research Press.

Whyman, R. (2011). *The Stanislavsky System of Acting: Legacy and Influence in Modern Performance*. Cambridge: Cambridge University Press.

Worthen, W. B. (1997). Shakespeare's auteurs: directing authority. In W. B. Worthen, *Shakespeare and the Authority of Performance* (pp. 45–94). Cambridge: Cambridge University Press.

Zon, B. (2011). *Shkola Borisa Zona (The School of Boris Zon)*. St Petersburg: St Petersburg Theatre Institute.

Index